Breaking Negative
Thinking Patterns

Breaking Negative Thinking Patterns

A Schema Therapy Self-Help and Support Book

Gitta Jacob, Hannie van Genderen
and Laura Seebauer

WILEY Blackwell

This edition first published 2015
© 2011 Beltz Psychologie in der Verlagsgruppe
Beltz • Weinheim Basel

Registered Office
John Wiley & Sons, Ltd, The Atrium, Southern Gate, Chichester, West Sussex,
PO19 8SQ, UK

Editorial Offices
350 Main Street, Malden, MA 02148-5020, USA
9600 Garsington Road, Oxford, OX4 2DQ, UK
The Atrium, Southern Gate, Chichester, West Sussex, PO19 8SQ, UK

For details of our global editorial offices, for customer services, and for information
about how to apply for permission to reuse the copyright material in this book please
see our website at www.wiley.com/wiley-blackwell.

The right of Gitta Jacob, Hannie van Genderen and Laura Seebauer to be identified as
the authors of this work has been asserted in accordance with the UK Copyright,
Designs and Patents Act 1988.

Library of Congress Cataloging-in-Publication data applied for.

Hardback ISBN: 9781118877722
Paperback ISBN: 9781118877715

A catalogue record for this book is available from the British Library.

Cover image: Daniel Viéné, *Visages Multiples*; courtesy of foxx galerie, Zurich,
www.foxxgalerie.com. Background © RapidEye / iStockphoto

Set in 11/14pts Minion by SPi Publisher Services, Pondicherry, India

Printed in Singapore by C.O.S. Printers Pte Ltd

Contents

Preface

Are you familiar with the experience of negative thinking patterns keeping you from attaining your personal goals? With this book we want to help you understand yourself, your feelings, and your personal patterns better. Your negative thinking patterns are the "beaten track" which you have walked many times. If you want to find new ways, you should understand the origins of your beaten track and why you take it again and again. The first part of this book is all about understanding negative thinking patterns, and the related emotions and behaviors. In the second part we will explain in detail how you can change these patterns, if you consider a change necessary or reasonable.

We base our explanations on the so-called Schema Mode approach. This is the latest development in Schema Therapy, which was developed by Jeffery Young and colleagues in New York (2006) and is rapidly spreading around the globe. Many therapists are enthusiastic about schema therapy, as it integrates experiences and techniques from various therapeutic approaches very effectively. Not only thoughts but also feelings are taken into consideration, and current problems are of interest as well as their origin in childhood. This usually gives clients the impression of work being done on the "core" of their problems in an easy and understandable way. In work with schema modes, clients and therapists are at eye-level. Both parties are looking for better ways to meet clients' needs.

In this book we try to go through the Schema Mode approach in an understandable way for anyone who is interested. We want to encourage you to change your patterns in such a way that negative feelings will weaken and positive feelings get more space in your life. To attain this goal, you will need to reduce disadvantageous coping strategies for negative feelings. You can use this book either as a self-help book or as assistance to a (Schema-) therapy. Psychological technical terms which may not be familiar to you are printed in **bold** and explained in the Glossary. You can download and print all worksheets from the book's website (www.wiley.com\go\Jacob\breakingnegativethoughtpatterns). More detailed instructions are provided at the end of the book.

This book project is part of a long-standing cooperation and exchange program of the University of Freiburg (Germany), the Regionale Instelling voor Ambulante Geestelijke Gezondheidszorg (RIAGG) in Maastricht and the University of Maastricht (Netherlands). This cooperation, which offered us many interesting insights and common projects, has been a pleasure throughout its duration. We thank Darren Reed and his colleagues from Wiley Blackwell for their effective and committed support. Claudia Styrsky drew the wonderful cartoons in this book – we could not get enough of them! Last but not least we say thanks to our husbands and families for being so tolerant (again) to help us devote so many week-ends and so much precious free time to this project!

Hamburg, Maastricht und Freiburg, Autumn 2014
Gitta Jacob, Hannie van Genderen, Laura Seebauer

Credit for Images

Illustrations are by Claudia Styrsky, München.

1

Introduction

Case Example "Exclusion"

Carol is a 34-year-old mother of a 4-year-old son, in a stable relationship. She works part-time as a bank assistant. She could be quite satisfied with her life, but minor incidents sometimes trigger severe feelings of exclusion or rejection. This may happen, for example, when her colleagues who work full-time make an "insider joke" she doesn't get. Most often, she reacts by drawing back from them. But she may also respond like a stroppy child to her colleagues, in particular when she is having a bad day anyway. Then she is not only annoyed by her colleagues, but also feels ashamed of her own reaction.

Carol has had this kind of problem all her life… maybe it has something to do with her childhood. Because of her father's frequent job changes, she was forced to move and start all over again several times. Facing a new school class, she often made the experience of feeling excluded. At the age of 12, she even experienced severe mobbing in school.

Does that sound familiar to you? Persistent patterns you just cannot get rid of? The same kind of feelings mixing up your life over and over again?

Breaking Negative Thinking Patterns: A Schema Therapy Self-Help and Support Book,
First Edition. Gitta Jacob, Hannie van Genderen and Laura Seebauer.
© 2011 Beltz Psychologie in der Verlagsgruppe
Beltz • Weinheim Basel. Published 2015 by John Wiley & Sons, Ltd.

If you want to change your patterns, you should first understand and recognize which patterns are bothering you right now in your daily life. Find out how these patterns developed over your life and why they are so persistent. In the first part of this book we explain how you can explore the origins of your patterns. You will also discover your real **needs** and how you can meet them better.

In Part II we will introduce methods to change your patterns step by step and in the way that you want. You can either deal with this by yourself, using the advice in this book, or, if and when this seems too difficult, you might consider seeking help from a therapist.

The therapy that's aiming to change your patterns is called schema therapy. The central concept in schema therapy is called "schema mode" or simply "Mode." A Mode is a persistent pattern of behaving and feeling that always causes the same type of problems. In fact, it is a state of mind that is connected to bad experiences in your youth or childhood.

In this book we will explain the schema Modes we know about and the ways that you can change them. You can use this book both as a self-help guide and as a support during a schema therapy. If you decide to change your Modes by yourself we recommend that you get someone you trust to discuss your patterns with you. We also recommend that you read this book step by step. Think about each chapter you read before going ahead. In this way you will learn to deal better with difficult situations, your negative feelings will diminish and you will fulfill your needs in a healthier way.

1.1   What Is Schema Therapy?

Schema therapy is one of the latest advances in psychotherapy. It is a development of cognitive behavior therapy, combining ideas from various psychotherapeutic approaches. Box 1.1 lists psychotherapy approaches that have been influential on schema therapy.

Box 1.1: **Approaches That Have Influenced Schema Therapy**

Cognitive behavioral therapy: Focusing on changes in thoughts and behavior in concrete, current life problems.

Depth psychology: Most psychological problems have their origin in experiences in childhood and youth.

Psychodrama and Gestalt therapy: Techniques to change problematic **emotions**.

Humanistic therapy/ Client-centered therapy: Focusing on human needs and on their importance for mental health.

Emotions play the most important role in schema therapy. Both positive and negative childhood experiences form our adult emotional reactions. Imagine that you have been humiliated as a child, because your clothes were different or your nose was extraordinarily big. If you often felt rejected and humiliated as a child, it's very likely that you will easily feel rejected or humiliated as an adult, too – even if nobody means to make you suffer this way. Such feelings typically lead to many problems: for instance, you might not make contact with others easily and thus not be able to establish healthy and close relationships; or you might react aggressively to prevent further humiliation, even if your action is not at all appropriate.

Therefore, the very first step of schema therapy is always to understand your negative feelings and their origin in your biography. Then, all current negative consequences of these feelings and childhood experiences are explored. The second step is to support you in changing your feelings and your dysfunctional behaviors. Thus, you will more satisfied and better able to fulfill your needs in a healthy and appropriate way.

1.2   Understanding the Origin of Your Patterns

A basic principle of the Mode concept is that everyone experience themselves differently at different moments. While you may feel very healthy and relaxed in one moment, you may feel vulnerable and sad in another. In some other situation you may rather be emotionally cold and feel nothing. Such different states are called "Modes." In schema therapy we define the following Modes:

- **Vulnerable and Angry Child Modes**. Most people are familiar with feelings of weakness, inferiority, sadness or intense rage, defiance or anger, in which they do not feel grown up. In schema therapy such states are called "Child Modes." We call them Child Modes because we assume that when important needs are not met in someone's childhood, they will have emotional parts that cannot grow up.
- **Dysfunctional Parent Modes**. People with intense Child Modes often tend to devalue themselves or to put excessive pressure upon themselves. These Modes are called Dysfunctional Parent Modes, as they have often been "modeled" by devaluing or abusive parents, or **bullying** class mates or siblings. The term *parent* in Parent Modes does not only relate to real parents, but also to any other important maladaptive attachment figure.
- **Coping Modes**. When someone is affected by negative feelings they tend to use one or more favored strategies to reduce those feelings or to hide them from others. The technical term for such psychological "survival strategies" is "Coping Mode." Such **coping** includes avoidant behaviors like social retreat or cannabis use in order to calm down negative feelings. Another way of coping with negative feelings is to behave aggressively or excessively self-confidently when actually feeling weak or inferior.
- **Healthy Adult Mode**. Of course we do not only have dysfunctional or immature modes: we also have healthy parts

with high-level functioning, healthy connections with other people, and positive emotions. The part that is able to organize your life, solve problems and take care of good relationships is called the "Healthy Adult Mode."

- **Happy Child Mode**. All people – both children and adults – have a need for fun, happiness and easiness. The Happy Child Mode is related to these feelings.

1.2.1   *Recognizing your Modes*

The first part of this book is all about becoming familiar with your Modes. It will describe and explain all the Modes. It includes many examples illustrating how to detect Modes in yourself and in others. We will find out how strong the different Modes are in *your* life. How did they develop in your life and why are some Modes more significant than others? We will focus on how your Modes make you feel and what type of situations cause them to pop up.

1.2.2   *Changing your Modes*

In the second part of the book you will learn strategies and exercises which can help you to change your Modes. The general aim is to enable you to cope with difficult situations in the way that suits you. You'll get to know your own needs better and learn how to fulfill them. These exercises and changes are related to three different levels of human experience:

- **Thoughts (Cognitive level)**. On the cognitive level it's most relevant to learn everything about your Modes and to reflect on the appropriateness of the cognitions related to your Modes. On this level you also work out realistic plans about what you want to change. Protocols and worksheets will guide and help you with this.
- **Feelings (Emotional level)**. You will find many suggestions on how to change distressing emotions. Imagery exercises are powerful emotional techniques. In these exercises you imagine yourself in a certain situation, and think about what you need and what you want to change. Next, you imagine that

you behave in a certain way to change the situation. The influence of this exercise on emotions is much stronger than merely thinking about the same issue.

- **Behaviors (Behavioral level)**. Behavior changes usually follow work with cognitions and emotions. The book will offer many examples and suggestions on how to change persistent behavior patterns in your life.

Of course, every person is unique, and your Modes differ from other people's. You will take different things out of this book than someone else will. Maybe you just want to get some information about schema therapy. Or maybe you want to try to find out how the Mode perspective applies to you. Maybe you suffer from an emotional problem, or you've been thinking about changing the way you behave in certain situations. You'll find several worksheets in the book which should help you in working out your Modes. But please be aware that this book is not a replacement for the psychotherapy you may need if you suffer from a serious mental illness!

We hope that this book will help you find out more about yourself and your Modes. Have fun on your "inner journey"!

Part I

Become Familiar with Your Modes

2

Child Modes

Everyone feels or acts like a child sometimes. However, most of us manage to control our childlike behavior in situations in which it would be inappropriate. Child Modes are a way of perceiving the world and other people that resembles the perception of children. Children have difficulty appreciating or adopting other people's perspective when experiencing strong emotions. An adult in a Child Mode has very similar feelings. Further, when you are in a Child Mode your reactions towards others can resemble the behavior of a child. Like a child, you may find it hard to control your impulses: you may start crying in a conversation with your boss, or you may slam the door in a fight with your partner.

Child Modes are active when we experience strong emotions that are not sufficiently explained by the current situation. When we are in a Child Mode feelings of sadness, anger, shame, or loneliness are exaggerated; it can be very difficult to calm down.

Child Modes are typically triggered when we feel rejected, left alone, or put under pressure. In such situations, the fulfillment of basic human needs like closeness, safety, or autonomy seems to

Breaking Negative Thinking Patterns: A Schema Therapy Self-Help and Support Book, First Edition. Gitta Jacob, Hannie van Genderen and Laura Seebauer.
© 2011 Beltz Psychologie in der Verlagsgruppe
Beltz • Weinheim Basel. Published 2015 by John Wiley & Sons, Ltd.

Box 2.1: Basic Emotional Needs

Basic emotional needs are important for all human beings. However, they can differ in their intensity. In schema therapy we assume five categories of basic emotional needs (Young, Klosko, & Weishaar, 2006)

1. Attachment and safety: You need to feel close to others. The need for attachment comprises safety, stability, attention, love, and acceptance by others.
2. Independence, competence, and identity: You need to have an idea of what makes you the person you are and what you are good at.
3. Freedom to express your important needs and feelings.
4. Spontaneity, fun, and playing.
5. Realistic boundaries: It is especially important for children to know their limits and to accept reasonable boundaries set by others.

People with psychological problems often find it difficult to get these emotional needs met.

---

be threatened (Box 2.1), even though this may objectively not be the case. Maybe your friend cancelled a date for the movies you had been looking forward to. If you react with a Child Mode, you may feel very disappointed, unloved, abandoned, or angry. From a more adult perspective you may be able to understand your friend's reasons for cancelling the date and you know that she usually cares a lot about you. Nevertheless, you are overwhelmed with strong feelings, start to cry, or retreat to your bed.

People suffering from emotional problems usually experience Child Modes particularly intensely. Small triggers can evoke strong negative feelings, even if the incident is trivial from a more objective perspective. Think of a colleague who did not compliment your new haircut. Most likely your colleague just did not notice or did not care because he was busy. If you have a strong Vulnerable Child Mode, you may feel alone and unloved. In this chapter we will explain why Child Modes show up so easily in some people.

Three types of Child Mode. The schema therapy model proposes three different types of Child Mode. The *Vulnerable Child Mode* is associated with depressed or anxious feelings such as shame, loneliness, anxiety, sadness, or threat. The second type is the so-called *Angry or Impulsive Child Mode*. In this Mode one usually feels rage, anger, impulsivity, or defiance. Impulsive behaviors appear when someone acts out of the moment without considering the possible negative consequences of his or her action. As an example, a man who was criticized by his boss feels angry and hurt: an impulsive reaction would be risky driving on the way home. The third type of child Mode is the *Happy Child Mode*. We regard this as a healthy Mode: one feels curious and playful, and takes easygoing pleasure in games and activities.

If one or more of these Modes sound familiar to you, it might be helpful for you to come up with your own name for it, such as "small Lisa" for the Vulnerable Child Mode or "pigheaded Tom" for the Angry Child Mode. That will help you to make contact with your child Mode when it comes up.

Everybody experiences feelings of sadness and rage from time to time. How can you decide if a child Mode is active and not just "normal" feelings?

Obviously, everyone knows the feelings related to child Modes very well. The significant difference between "normal feelings" and Child Modes is that child Modes are activated by very small incidents. The intensity of negative emotions seems disproportionate to the event. Moreover, it is really hard for a person in a child Mode to control those feelings and the related reactions.

Figure 2.1   Child Modes

Table 2.1   Naming Child Modes

Vulnerable Child Mode	*Angry or Impulsive Child Mode*	*Happy Child Mode*
Your own name for this Mode:	Your own name for this Mode:	Your own name for this Mode:
Related feelings:	Related feelings:	Related feelings:
• Anxiety	• Irritated	• Playfulness
• Sadness	• Rage	• Easiness
• Loneliness	• Anger	• Curiosity
• Despair	• Impulsivity	• Fun
• Helplessness	• Defiance	• Lightheartedness
• Shame	• Stubbornness	• Safety
• Abandonment	• Lack of discipline	• Confident
• Dependence	• Spoilt	
• Abused		
• Humiliated		

2.1   Vulnerable Child Modes

Vulnerable child Modes go along with all types of sad or anxious emotions. Most people can easily name the feeling which troubles them most; the experience of mixed feelings is also very common. The following examples will give you hints about what to focus on when you wish to get in contact with your own Vulnerable Child Mode. They might also help you understand which situations Vulnerable Child Modes usually appear in. Please keep in mind that the following examples do not aspire to completeness. Your child Mode may be associated with different feelings.

Abandonment or instability. If you suffer from strong feelings of abandonment, you will often have a sense of being abandoned by others or you fear that you will soon be abandoned. Even in the company of close friends or family members you may happen to experience feelings of loneliness. People with strong feelings of loneliness or abandonment often experienced some kind of desertion in their childhood or youth. Maybe a parent left the family, an important attachment figure died, or they had to live in a succession of foster families that rejected them over and over again.

Case Example "Abandonment"

Sophia is a 34-year-old middle school teacher. She suffers from anxiety attacks and feelings of dissociation and alienation from her body. These problems occur when she has to return to her own apartment after having spent time with her family at the place where she grew up. She feels lonely and abandoned in such situations, even though she has friends in the place where she lives. She tells her therapist that she does not feel close to other people and that all her relationships seem to her to be superficial. When discussing these issues she suddenly feels very sad and gets the feeling that no one will ever stay with her. The therapist suggests that this could be related to Sophia's repeated loss of a mother figure: her birth mother died when she was 2 years old, and her beloved stepmother died unexpectedly from a cerebral hemorrhage when Sophia was 16.

Social isolation. Some people lack the feeling of belonging to others. They feel isolated, as if they were cut off from the rest of the world. The origin of this feeling is very often an experience of being excluded, for example, by frequent moving or by membership in an unusual, restrictive religious community. Early exclusion from the family or the group of siblings can be traumatic as well. In adult life, seemingly unimportant social signals, such as the order of seating at a dinner party, can trigger the Mode of the excluded child.

Case Example "Isolation"

Megan moved a lot with her family when she was a child. She had always been the "new girl," didn't belong to her changing peer groups, and felt excluded. Today she attends university and has found some good friends. But when her fellow students make plans without explicitly including her, she readily feels excluded even when that is objectively not the case.

Mistrust and abuse. Mistrust goes along with a feeling of constant threat. You are always alert to signs of threat and have a suspicious attitude towards other people. People suffering from severe feelings of mistrust are always on their guard, sensing a need to avoid harm by other people. As with the emotions described above, the origin of mistrust most often lies in problematic childhood experiences. A woman who has been sexually abused as a child may become panicky merely from the sound of keys in the door. As another example, think of someone who was bullied on his way to school. As an adult this person cannot stand it if someone walks closely behind him.

Defectiveness and shame. Shame is another possible dominant feeling of a Vulnerable Child Mode. Often feelings of being deficient, bad, inferior, or unwanted are linked. You feel as if you

---

Case Example "Mistrust and abuse"

Astrid is very frightened of the dark. She always sleeps with the light on. When her husband is not at home she usually stays at a friend's place overnight. As soon as she notices an unfamiliar noise outside, her body stiffens and she gets panicky. Every shadow on the street makes her feel anxious and helpless. As a child she suffered from the violent temper of her father. He used to hit her and her brothers and sisters randomly if something upset him. Her mother couldn't protect her as the father also beat her.

---

are not worth the love, attention, and respect of others. Instead you may feel horribly ashamed of the way you are. People with these feelings have frequently been the victims of devaluing comments or humiliating treatment in their childhood or adolescence.

Case Example "Defectiveness and Shame"

Daniel's teacher in high school had a few favorite students. Daniel was not one of them. He was very insecure during puberty because he had grown very fast and often felt awkward and behaved clumsily. This teacher repeatedly exposed him to ridicule when he stumbled or behaved awkwardly in any other way. The ensuing laughter of his classmates was extremely humiliating for Daniel. Twenty years later he is a successful IT counselor. On one occasion he accidentally stumbled over the flip chart in a meeting and his colleagues started laughing. Immediately Daniel felt rising feelings of shame and helplessness and escaped to the toilet where it took him several minutes to calm down.

Emotional deprivation. People suffering from emotional deprivation usually feel that their childhood was "on the whole, all right." But somehow they still did not get the feeling of really being cared for and loved. They lack security, closeness, and attachment. As adults they do not necessarily report constant emotional distress. They do not really miss anything. Still they feel like they don't matter for other people, and this is a painful experience.

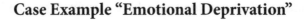

Case Example "Emotional Deprivation"

Steven is a 38-year-old sales marketer who likes his job and fulfills it to his bosses' satisfaction. His marriage is happy and he also has some friends. Still he can't get rid of the feeling of never being close to others and loved by them. He tries really hard to get proof of affection from others, both in his job and in his private life. Although there are plenty of people who do like him and let him know it, he can hardly ever feel their affection. Steven says that his childhood was "all right." His parents were always very busy and often absent. He often felt that it was too much for his parents to take care of their children on top of everything else.

Dependency or incompetence. When you feel unable to do anything independently and do not dare to decide things by yourself, you behave like a dependent child. For children it is normal to depend on parents for important decisions, such as the choice of their school. But if your parents did not stimulate you to make your own choices, even if at times they had different preferences than you did, you may remain dependent on other people. You may not even know what your preferences are. In adult life you still think that your parents or your partner are responsible for your life.

Case Example "Dependency and Incompetence"

Marjorie lived with her parents till the age of 24, when she married Bob. He has a full-time job and she does the housekeeping. She always worked in her parents' shop, and she doesn't dare to look for another job. She lives near her parents and visits them every day. She asks her parents or Bob for advice about everything. She asks her mother what she should eat, how to decorate her house, and even how to dress. All the other decisions she leaves to Bob.

2.1.1 Get in contact with your own Vulnerable Child Mode

By reading the case examples you might already have got an idea of what a Vulnerable Child Mode can feel like. The following points will help you to check whether you have a Vulnerable Child Mode as well. If you agree quite strongly with one of the statements, this might be the first clue. If you agree only weakly, you probably know these feelings but they don't cause you serious distress.

- I often feel completely alone.
- I feel weak and helpless.
- I have the feeling that no one loves me.

Do you agree with one or more of these statements? If you often feel sad, abandoned, or anxious without a particular reason it's probably because of a Vulnerable Child Mode. Very often there is a link between this Mode and your personal history.

If you want to get to know your Vulnerable Child Mode more closely, the following questions may be helpful. You can also use Worksheet 2, "My Vulnerable Child Mode":

- What are common triggers for my Vulnerable Child Mode? Which situations does it appear in?
- What feelings do I experience in this Mode?
- What thoughts typically come up when I am in this Mode?
- What memories or mental images are associated with my Vulnerable Child Mode?
- How does my body feel in this Mode?
- How I do I typically act in this Mode? How do I treat other people?

If you try to be aware of your Vulnerable Child Mode in your everyday life, you will soon understand it much better. You'll learn what makes it turn up over and over again. You may use Worksheet 1, your "Mode overview worksheet" to fill in these points.

Worksheet 1: My Mode Overview

My Mode Overview
My Child Mode(s)
My Parent Mode(s)
My Coping Mode(s)
My Healthy Adult Mode

Worksheet 2: My Vulnerable Child Mode

My Vulnerable Child Mode
My name for this Mode (e.g. Little Lisa):
1. How can I realize that my Vulnerable Child Mode is present?
What is **triggering** my vulnerable child Mode?
What **feelings** do I usually have in this Mode?
What **thoughts** tend to come up in this Mode?
What **memories** are associated/get triggered?
How does my **body** feel in this Mode?
How do I usually **behave** in this Mode?
2. Do I tend to switch Modes (e.g. to Angry Child Mode or to a Coping Mode) when I am in the Vulnerable Child Mode? To which one?
3. What are my actual **needs** when I am in the Vulnerable Child Mode?
4. Are my needs met by my behavior (e.g. need for closeness)?

2.1.2   Detecting Vulnerable Child Modes in others

When you sense that somebody feels very easily frightened, threatened, unstable, or is close to tears, this hints at a vulnerable Child Mode in that person. Another sign can be a constant urge for reassurance, for example, "Are you *really* sure that you want me to join you and your friends tonight?" Another clear indicator for a Vulnerable Child Mode is black and white thinking, where the world is split into two parts – good and bad. For example, your friend is convinced that you are completely on her partner's side in a conflict after you made a small critical remark on her behavior.

Do you remember any situation in which one of your friends, family members, or colleagues seemed to be in a Vulnerable Child Mode? Do you understand what made him or her switch into that Mode? How did he or she behave in the Vulnerable Child Mode? Do you have a clue on the person's needs in that situation? How did you feel yourself towards that person, and how did you react?

Maybe you felt compassionate and were able to show it. It is also possible that you felt overstrained, helpless, or irritated because arguments and consolidation didn't seem to help. If you remember your own feelings or reactions towards this person, it makes it easier for you to understand how other people feel when you are in your Vulnerable Child Mode.

2.2   Angry and Impulsive Child Modes

The so-called Angry or Impulsive Child Modes resemble the Vulnerable Child Mode in that they, too, do not make you feel adult. They are often triggered when you feel that your needs are not respected. However, unlike the Vulnerable Child Mode, they are related to the so-called "hot" feelings, like anger and rage. Your behavior in this Mode might be angry or enraged but also defiant or undisciplined. Spoilt behavior is also possible in this Mode.

What is the common ground of these feelings and actions? Most importantly they all express needs in an exaggerated or inappropriate way. Either the reaction is extremely emotional, with excessive anger or rage, or it is inappropriately spoilt, defiant, or impulsive. It is important to understand that the underlying needs are legitimate; it is absolutely normal to get angry when your needs are not met! However, the behavior associated with this Mode is often inappropriate. For convenience and clarity we will from now on use the term "Angry Child Mode" to encompass *all* the feelings discussed above. Later on you will learn more about the different shades of this Mode.

Very frequently the Angry Child Mode goes along with the Vulnerable Child Mode which you got to know in the previous section. Maybe you get very angry when a friend cancels your date for the movies. Afterwards, feelings of sadness, loneliness, or abandonment might crop up. In this case an Angry Child Mode is triggered and followed by a Vulnerable Child Mode. It can also be the other way around. You may feel lonely and abandoned at first and then get worked up into anger or rage. Many people experience mixed feelings when they face the other person. Imagine that you want to confront your friend with your anger, but as you start talking, you also start crying. Here, Angry and Vulnerable Child Modes are both present at the same moment.

In the group of Angry Child Modes a lot of different feelings can play a role. It is important to understand the dominant angry child feeling. Is it "blind rage" or do you rather feel defiant or pigheaded? Are you angry because you feel you're being treated unfairly? Or are you too spoilt to accept limits that are actually valid for everybody? The following list depicts emotions people experience in Angry Child Modes. Of course it is also possible to experience a mix of these emotions.

Anger. When anger is dominant you experience intense annoyance or strong frustration when emotional needs (e.g., for acceptance or attention) are not met. This anger might come out in a very strong way, for example, as hurtful claims or sharp criticism. You may tend to "swallow" your anger. However, others may still sense it, even if it doesn't come out so strongly.

Case Example "Angry Child Mode"

Matthew, a 41-year-old software engineer, tries hard to do everything right for everybody. He is determined always to give a good impression. At the same time he feels easily hurt, rejected, and often believes that he's being treated unfairly. As a child he'd been harshly criticized and had rarely experienced love and attention. This is probably why criticism is his "sore spot." When he thinks he's being criticized he becomes very angry. He reacts with sarcastic answers or offending e-mails, even if someone merely tried to help him with a suggestion.

Rage. When rage is dominant, your feelings in this Mode are very intense. In an Enraged Child Mode you may get completely out of control. You may destroy things or even hurt other people. The enraged child is out of control, hits everything in its way, screams, and defends itself furiously against (assumed) attacks. Anger and rage are very similar feelings. You can distinguish between them by their emotional intensity. Rage is more intense and harder to control than anger.

Case Example "Enraged Child Mode"

Florence works the night shift as a nurse to earn a living for herself and her three kids. She feels constantly overstrained by her work and the responsibility for her family. Often she is completely exhausted and frustrated when she returns home from work. When she sees her children's jackets and school bags thrown carelessly onto the floor, she feels rage rising. She then slams the door and swears loudly. Her husband often says that she is overreacting and asks her to be more relaxed but that does not help her. The next small lapse brings on her rage again.

In her childhood, Florence was often alone because her mother was at work; her father was a severe alcoholic who did not take care of anything. He often had extremely scary outbursts of rage. Florence was a bright child who soon learned to be very independent – but ever since her childhood she has felt rage from "always having it hard."

Defiance. When being defiant you feel angry but you don't express it directly. However, other people usually get a clear sense of your anger because you are in a defiant retreat or you're behaving in a passive-aggressive way. People who experienced their autonomy not being respected as children often develop a defiant Angry Child Mode ("of course they don't ask me"). The dominant emotion of a Defiant Child Mode is often a feeling of injustice.

Impulsivity. You act impulsively when you go for your (short-term) needs without considering negative consequences for yourself or other people. Typical examples are spending more money than you can afford on unnecessary things, overuse of drugs or alcohol, unprotected sex, or eating attacks. The common feature of these behaviors is that current desires are fulfilled no matter what. An observer would probably consider the behavior inappropriate or unnecessary. Very often, the person with the Impulsive Child Mode would agree later on and regret their impulsive behavior. However, when the Impulsive Child Mode is activated, the desire is dominant.

Case Example "Impulsive Child Mode"

Susie is 21 years old and recently moved to another city to start her studies. She enjoys student life a lot, goes out every night, drinks a lot and often ends up having sex with new acquaintances. When she is sober she is often shocked by her own behavior because she sometimes does not even use protection, risking pregnancy and sexually transmitted disease. But when the next party is on, she doesn't want to worry and the same things happen again. After some time, Susie gets into increasing trouble as she rarely attends her course and spends way more money than she can afford.

Susie grew up in a rather chaotic family. Her parents held the view that the kids should be allowed to try anything and did not set any limits for her. Moreover, because her parents were often absent, Susie was partly raised by her older sister, who had a similar lifestyle.

Pamperedness. Being impulsive and being spoilt are overlapping patterns. However, while people with an Impulsive Child Mode are usually critical about their impulsive behaviors in the long term, people with a Spoilt Child Mode find it normal and perfectly acceptable that they don't have to bear the same responsibilities as others. Very often, they have been spoilt in their childhood, too. Most likely they feel offended when others do not tolerate their demands and set them limits, though Spoilt Child Mode often does not go along with strong emotions.

Case Example "Spoilt Child Mode"

Ethan is in a loving relationship with his girlfriend Lucy. Lucy is very understanding and supports Ethan in pursuing his own interests. In return she expects him to do his share of the housekeeping work. Nevertheless, he frequently fails to fulfill his everyday obligations such as shopping in the supermarket. Lucy sometimes gets very annoyed by that. When she tries to confront him he retreats to his computer and stops talking to her for several hours. Ethan reacts defiantly in those situations and Lucy cannot talk to him about either the supermarket or his defiant behavior.

When Lucy gets to know Ethan's mother she starts understanding the origins of this behavior. His mother has been pampering him since infancy and still fulfills all his wishes. In return she does not expect him either to take on any responsibilities or take care of other people's needs. On the other hand, she interferes in personal affairs without being asked. Now Lucy can see how Ethan developed his defiant and spoilt attitude.

Lack of discipline. People with an Undisciplined Child Mode are hardly able to complete boring or annoying duties, it is very hard for them to take on normal, everyday responsibilities. Issues are neglected which are highly important to the pursuit of certain life goals. People with a lack of discipline are not always spoilt in the sense that they think that others will do their job for them, although that may happen, too. But often they simply live with important jobs not being done. They never learned to stand the frustration that goes along with boring duties. In the worst cases, such a Mode can cause chronic, severe problems. Sometimes people use the term "**procrastination**" to describe these phenomena.

Case Example "Undisciplined Child Mode"

For Ethan (see also case example "Spoilt Child Mode") it is very hard to complete boring assignments that are important for his studies in law. He has difficulty studying regularly and completing his thesis. Even when he starts working on his thesis, he usually ends up playing video games, surfing the Internet, or watching television. Lucy often thinks that it was not to Ethan's advantage that he was a "bright kid" in school because he missed the opportunity to get used to being disciplined, completing boring assignments, and taking responsibility.

2.2.1   Get in contact with your own Angry or Impulsive Child Mode

Of course, not every angry or impulsive action should be considered as part of a highly dysfunctional Mode. Anger is a normal feeling indicating a violation of your rights or limits, and everyone gets angry now and then. It is even a problem if you cannot feel anger. There are a lot of reasons for justified anger; also, most people delay annoying duties as long as possible. And, of course, most people are more likely to react with irritation when they are hungry or tired. Such reactions are not an Angry Child Mode.

We call a pattern an Angry Child Mode when somebody reacts frequently in one or more of the ways associated with the Mode, and when this pattern causes serious problems in his or her life. This would be the case if the Angry Child Mode puts the job or relationship in danger because other people feel offended or threatened.

The following statements can help you determine whether this applies to you. Please take into account that questionnaires only can give a hint. Your personal appraisal counts most!

- When I get angry I cannot control myself and lose containment.
- I do what I want no matter how other people feel or think about it.
- I break rules and regret it afterwards.
- I think that normal rules don't apply to me.

Section 2.1 (Vulnerable Child Mode) was all about feeling sad, weak, lonely, or inferior. Experiencing the feelings of the

Vulnerable Child Mode can be very painful. In contrast, if you are in Angry or Impulsive Child Mode you often feel strong and powerful. It can be a great feeling to put others in their place. But then you might feel ashamed afterwards, or an outburst of anger can be followed by feelings of sadness and abandonment.

Particularly in Spoilt and Impulsive Child Modes, feelings are often not very intense. In these Modes it's all about granting yourself what you want (or do not want to do…). Just as children may feel great when behaving in a spoilt way, people usually feel quite good in this Mode. However, these Child Modes cause long-term problems, such as financial debt, relationship problems, and bad grades in school (see also Box 2.2 "Problematic Behaviors").

Box 2.2: Problematic Behaviors

Psychologists talk about "problem behaviors" if a certain behavior is comfortable or pleasant in the short term but causes problems in the long term. Conversely, "healthy" behaviors are often unpleasant or boring in the short term and pay off in the long run.

Here are some examples of problem behaviors:

- Smoking: In the short term you enjoy it, in the long run it might cause sickness or death. The opposed healthy behavior "quit smoking" is extremely difficult in the short run, but saves your long-term health.
- Eating too much: In the short term it is pleasant and enjoyable, but causes long term overweight and health problems. The alternate behavior "eat reasonably and exercise" is difficult to hang on to in the moment but pays in the long run.
- Impulsive, Spoilt, and Undisciplined Child Modes often include typical problematic behaviors. They feel good in the short term but you can already see the problems on the horizon.

Other people might find your Angry or Impulsive Child Mode more distressing than you do. A hint about that could be someone telling you that your behavior is inappropriate, that you are spoilt, or that your defiance is a pain. If you've heard something like that more than once you should be alarmed – probably there's some truth in it!

Try to think this pattern through for the following "problematic behaviors": delaying the annual tax declaration; postponing a visit to the dentist. For the Angry and Impulsive Child Modes it is, again, very important to understand how they are triggered, how they make you feel, and where they stem from in your biography. The following questions might be relevant to help you understand your Angry Child Mode better:

- What are typical triggers of your Angry or Impulsive Child Mode? In which situations does it get activated?
- What feelings are dominant in that Mode? Is it more about frustration, anger, rage, or defiance? Do you feel more strong or weak in this Mode?
- Is your Angry Child Mode usually followed by a Vulnerable Child Mode? Or is it the other way round?
- What thoughts are typical of this Mode? If you feel unjustly treated – what is the injustice?
- What memories and mental images are related to this Mode? You may have to dive into your fantasy to find that out.
- How do you typically act in this Mode? How do you react to others and how do others react to you? Does that remind you of something in your childhood?

Worksheet 3, "My Angry/Impulsive Child Mode," can help you to understand this Mode and its origin in your biography better.

2.2.2   Detecting Angry or Impulsive Child Modes in others

Obviously your first clue of an Angry Child Mode is the display of rage or anger. Only *inappropriate or exaggerated* anger would be considered an expression of an Angry Child Mode. Maybe

Worksheet 3: My Angry / Impulsive Child Mode

My Angry / Impulsive Child Mode
My name for this Mode (e.g. Firebrand):
1. How can I realize that my Angry / Impulsive Child Mode is present?
What is **triggering** my Angry / Impulsive Child Mode?
What **feelings** do I usually have in this Mode?
What **thoughts** tend to come up in this Mode?
What **memories** are associated / get triggered?
How does my **body** feel in this Mode?
How do I usually **behave** in this Mode?
2. Do I tend to switch Modes (e.g. to Vulnerable Child Mode or a Coping Mode) when I am in the Angry Child Mode? To which one?
3. What are my actual **needs** when I am in the Angry Child Mode?
4. Are my needs met by my behavior (e.g. need for respect)?

Worksheet 4: Advantages and Disadvantages of My Angry / Impulsive Child Mode

Advantages and Disadvantages of My Angry / Impulsive Child Mode		
	Advantages	*Disadvantages*
Short-term		
Long-term		

you understand that somebody is frustrated, but still feel that his or her reaction is excessive and over the top. Somebody may be in an Angry Child Mode when he or she is extremely upset about small details. Some people cannot calm down their anger and keep talking about the same situation over and over again. Here an Angry Child Mode might be involved, too. Your reaction might be to think, "He really should get over it. There is no use in getting upset all over again." However, when you put this to the person this he or she may criticize you or start crying.

The following patterns indicate Impulsive, Spoilt, Defiant, or Undisciplined Child Modes. Maybe you are faced with someone who consistently takes your support and help for granted. Or you find it intolerable how defiant you partner gets when you want to talk about a problem in a quiet and sensible way. If you have thoughts like "that is so childish" or "is she really grown up?" it's usually Child Modes in action. If a person is in a Vulnerable Child Mode most people feel compassion for them whereas people in an Angry or Impulsive Child Mode provoke more aversive reactions. People feel annoyed or frustrated because they're trying to behave reasonably and the other person just keeps picking on them. It can be useful to ask yourself the following questions to understand this Mode in other people.

- Do you understand why the Angry Child Mode gets triggered?
- What do you think are the person's genuine needs right now? Very often anger display goes along with feeling excluded or rejected, and the genuine need behind the anger is closeness and social contact.
- How do you react to this Mode? What are your thoughts, feelings, and actions?
- To what extent are the genuine needs of the person expressed by the Angry Child Mode and fulfilled by the reactions of others to this Mode? Does the person succeed in getting his or her needs met?
- With regard to spoilt and impulsive Modes, do you have an idea about the origin of this Mode? Do parents or other important figures in the affected person's life tend to act in a spoilt or impulsive manner as well? Or has the person been pampered as a child?
- With regard to Angry and Enraged Child Modes, where do you think this Mode stems from? Were important parent figures angry or aggressive? Or did the person suffer from bad or unfair treatment in their childhood?

When someone is in an Angry or Impulsive Child Mode, you may also feel angry or frustrated and act accordingly. Another possibility is that you feel powerless or helpless facing their anger or complaints. Of course it is most helpful to discuss these questions directly with the respective person, especially if it is your partner or a good friend. But only discuss these issues when the person is in the Healthy Adult Mode (see Chapter 5).

2.3　Happy Child Mode

You are a lucky person if you already have a strong Happy Child Mode! This Mode goes along with fun, playfulness, lightheartedness, and curiosity. In the Happy Child Mode we do things that are funny and pleasant, like playing, visiting theme parks, or going to the cinema. You may dress up for carnival or just play a card game with your friends. In the Happy Child Mode we feel attached to other people and experience closeness with them.

A strong Happy Child Mode is protective for your mental health. The Angry and Vulnerable Child Modes are in many ways opposite to the Happy Child Mode, and are often intense in people with emotional problems. People with a strong Vulnerable Child Mode typically have weak Happy Child Modes and vice versa.

We assume that for many of our readers it is an important goal to strengthen and build up their Happy Child Mode. It can replace a vulnerable or Angry Child Mode. Of course, you should always try to keep a good balance. It would not be appropriate always to be in a Happy Child Mode. The Healthy Adult Mode should actually be your "default mode" (see Chapter 5). Nevertheless, it is very important to notice when you are feeling the need for fun and recovery from your everyday life. It is important to have a repertoire of activities promoting your Happy Child Mode for those situations. Thus you can balance moments of stress and frustration.

Case Examples "Happy Child Mode"

1.　Anne is a hard-working researcher. She and her husband take care of their three kids. Anne has got a very tight time schedule and often works late at night.

Luckily, she has got some activities that bring on her Happy Child Mode easily. She has some close friends whom she meets every Friday night to play bridge. In this circle of friends she can completely let go and they have a lot of fun together. At the weekends she visits theme parks with her children and enjoys the roller coaster. In those situations she does not feel the burden of all her responsibilities. Without her Happy Child Mode Anne might be at risk of developing psychological problems like burnout or depression. If she had a strong Punitive Parent Mode (see Chapter 3), she would not allow herself those fun activities. She would miss the balance and would be at risk of falling into a vicious circle of stress and exhaustion.

2. Michael was educated as a childcare worker but then decided to study the field of education. Additionally, he works with young people in various circus projects in which he learns and teaches acrobatic tricks and vaudeville shows. Michael has made his Happy Child Mode his job and organizes public shows with the help of his friends. He is most fond of street improvisation theatre. Luckily, his wife has a secure job with a fixed income, which balances the financial insecurity that accompanies Michael's job. At some point in the future Michael wants to get a more secure job but for the moment he enjoys life as it is.

3. Emma is a 60-year-old teacher without children of her own. Nevertheless she loves children and has a strong bond to her nieces and nephews as well as the children of her close friends. Children love holidays at Aunt Emma's place. She visits toy stores and takes exciting trips with them. In summer Emma and the children can really get into playing with their new toys and the discoveries they make at their trips to the zoo.

2.3.1   Get in contact with your own Happy Child Mode

It is usually quite easy to identify your Happy Child Mode. You feel light and happy; you have fun and laugh a lot. Overall, you feel that the world is all right. You are connected with others and do not feel envious or jealous. The world and your life are shining in bright and friendly colors. The following statements belong to the Happy Child Mode:

- I feel accepted and loved.
- I am satisfied and relaxed.
- I trust most of the people around me.
- I am spontaneous and playful.

Many people find that their Happy Child Mode does not occur frequently or strongly enough. Because of that it is important to ask yourself the following questions.

- Which actions, situations, and persons trigger your Happy Child Mode?
- When did you last feel your Happy Child Mode? Think about the last week, when did you feel happy and lighthearted?
- What belongs to your Happy Child Mode? What is important? Are there certain people, special activities, or certain situations (like weekends or sunny weather)?
- Is there anything that makes it easier for you to get into your Happy Child Mode? Some people feel more relaxed after exercise, then they can start playful activities more easily.

You can use Worksheet 5, "My Happy Child Mode," to become familiar with your Happy Child Mode. But be aware that life is not perfect! Even if you feel that you never experience happy times, there may be opportunities that bring a little bit of Happy Child Mode into your life. It is all about getting to know your chances in life and then take one step after another. All items of information about your Happy Child Mode should be put in Worksheet 1, "My mode overview."

Worksheet 5: My Happy Child Mode

My Happy Child Mode
My name for this Mode (e.g. Happy Susie):
1. How can I realize that my Happy Child Mode is present?
What is **triggering** my Happy Child Mode?
What **feelings** do I usually have in this Mode?
What **thoughts** tend to come up in this Mode?
What **memories** are associated/get triggered?
How does my **body** feel in this Mode?
How do I usually **behave** in this Mode?

2.3.2   Detecting the Happy Child in others

This is a simple task as well. When you experience others sweeping you away with their good mood and their laughter, they probably have a strong Happy Child Mode. The Vulnerable and Angry Child Modes often scare others off, starting a vicious circle where others easily retreat. With the Happy Child Mode it's the other way around. People with a strong Happy Child Mode spread amusement and relaxation. Others like them and love to be around them. Thus, a virtuous circle is running. Your Happy Child Mode will draw other people to you and make you more popular. This will increase your sense of belonging. You will feel well and stable, which is a great basis for even more Happy Child Mode activation.

Case Example "Happy Child Mode"

Jessica is very successful in cultivating her Happy Child Mode in her life. She works as a management trainer and group therapist and is very good at her job. She also takes a lot of time for family activities like sports, games, and children's theater. She sends out good vibes that immediately attach people around her. She is particularly famous for her open laughter. When Jessica goes out with a group of friends the mood is significantly more fun and relaxed then without her. This leads to many invitations for parties or other social activities. Even her colleagues enjoy co-operation with her and try to enhance it because she always generates a good atmosphere.

2.4   Summary

In this chapter we described three types of Child Modes. The *Vulnerable Child Mode* is associated with depressed or anxious feelings such as shame, loneliness, anxiety, sadness or threat.

When your *Angry or Impulsive Child Mode* is triggered you experience rage, anger, impulsivity, or defiance. The *Happy Child Mode* makes you feel curious and playful, and take easygoing pleasure in games and activities. This Mode is a healthy Child Mode.

Everyone with persistent distressing negative patterns and feelings mixing up their life has at least a Vulnerable Child Mode. Besides that you may have an Angry or Impulsive Child Mode, but that is not always the case. The Happy Child Mode is mostly underdeveloped and rarely present. All information about your Child Modes can be put in Worksheet 1, the Mode Overview Worksheet.

In the next chapters you can discover how your "Dysfunctional (or damaging) Parent Modes" put pressure on you and make you feel unwanted or rejected. Next, you'll be introduced to different ways to deal with these difficult emotional experiences. We call these survival strategies to handle difficult or threatening situations "coping styles."

3

Dysfunctional Parent Modes

In this chapter you will learn more about the Modes putting pressure on you or making you feel unwanted or rejected – like an inner voice telling you over and over again that you are not smart or attractive enough to accomplish your goals and be accepted by others. The origin of such inner voices is usually in your childhood and adolescence – nobody dislikes him- or herself from birth. In most cases, somebody in the close environment of a child made it feel unwanted or "not good enough." These Modes are called "Dysfunctional Parent Modes" to underline that they contain early messages from other people. Dysfunctional is in this context defined as "damaging" or "not helpful."

Unfortunately the name "Dysfunctional Parent Mode" can be misleading, as it implies that it is always the fault of the parents when people cannot accept themselves. Such is the case for many people – parents do often play a significant role in the development of this Mode. Nevertheless, other people can also hurt you so badly that you turn out to have a strong "Punitive Parent Mode" later in life. Oftentimes, children are bullied and excluded from their class-mates. This can cause lifelong feelings of rejection. Within families it might be other persons than parents (like grandparents or sib-lings) who make a child feel bad or inadequate by criticizing, ignoring, or abusing him or her. However, it may be that only some parts of the parents' behavior were damaging, not everything they

Breaking Negative Thinking Patterns: A Schema Therapy Self-Help and Support Book,
First Edition. Gitta Jacob, Hannie van Genderen and Laura Seebauer.
© 2011 Beltz Psychologie in der Verlagsgruppe
Beltz • Weinheim Basel. Published 2015 by John Wiley & Sons, Ltd.

did. Maybe your parents loved you a lot and were able to show their love in many situations; but if they were very perfectionist in some areas, you may still have developed a so called "Demanding Parent Mode."

Despite all that, we decided to keep working with the term "Dysfunctional Parent Mode," as parents in most cases partly enabled these problems, or were at least not able to protect their children. For example, they did not prevent your brother or sister bullying you. Moreover, this term is used by schema therapists worldwide.

In the box below you will find three examples of Dysfunctional Parent Modes. Some cases represent Demanding Parent Modes, others Guilt-inducing or Punitive Parent Modes. Maybe you already have a clue about how these three Modes differ.

Case Examples "Dysfunctional Parent Modes"

1. When Aisha gets into an argument with her friend Helena, Helena sometimes stops talking to Aisha for a whole day and pretends that she doesn't exist. Aisha feels terribly unwanted and unloved (=*Vulnerable Child Mode*). At the same time, she blames herself for being egoistic and feels extreme pressure to please her friend, even if she thinks that her position in the argument was justified (=*Guilt-inducing Parent Mode*). Her friend's reaction reminds Aisha strongly of her own mother, who used to punish her by depriving her of love. Aisha always had strong feelings of guilt when she did not wholly comply with her mothers' wishes. Presumably that is why she is so vulnerable to those feelings.

2. Annabelle used to get punished sadistically in the Magdalene asylum where she grew up. When she stood up against the sisters, she was sometimes not allowed to

---

have dinner. Even many years later, Annabelle is not able to respond to someone who is in the wrong, because this would make her feel ashamed and full of self-hatred. Moreover, Annabelle is incapable of enjoying tasty food. When she is invited to a delicate dinner, she gets overwhelmed with shame. She simply feels not worthy of good food. The inner voice proclaiming "you are too bad to deserve good food" is a strong Punitive Parent Mode. Feelings of shame belong to Annabelle's Vulnerable Child Mode, since the sisters had exposed her to ridicule many times.

3. Freddie always was an overachiever in school, at university, and in his professional career. His accomplishments were praised by parents and teachers, but were taken for granted after some time. Today he is 28 years old and would like to spend more time with his girlfriend. However, it is very hard for him to leave work when there is something left to do. He feels strong pressure to do everything in time and never postpone an urgent job. Even when he leaves his office he cannot stop thinking about work; he cannot relax and enjoy his leisure time. There is a constant voice in his head telling him "you have to be perfect in everything you do." This is a Demanding Parent Mode focusing on achievement.

Dysfunctional Parent Modes and Vulnerable (sometimes also Angry) Child Modes often come together. Risky situations are negative events related to experiences of being rejected or being criticized. Such situations often trigger a Dysfunctional Parent Mode. This may be the case even if your "critics" are actually friends with a high opinion of you. An example would be the case of Aisha: rejection by a friend triggered her Guilt-inducing Parent Mode.

Perhaps you have the experience of your boss pointing out a mistake you've made. This may make you feel very bad, even though it is actually a completely normal thing to happen. If you have a strong Demanding Parent Mode, it will easily be triggered in such a situation. It may make you feel severely criticized and incapable. If your Demanding Parent Mode is really strong you may even be afraid of being fired, although the criticism was constructive and factual. These experiences are quite probably associated with feelings of helplessness or shame, depending on your experiences in childhood and youth. These feelings represent the Vulnerable Child Mode – an example of the way that Dysfunctional Parent Modes and Child Modes are often triggered together.

Nevertheless, we think that it's very important to treat the Child and Parent Modes separately. In the later chapters of this book you will learn that the schema therapy treatment for these two types of Modes is very different. Vulnerable Child Modes call for comforting and protection; you have to learn to take good care of them. Dysfunctional Parent Modes, on the other hand, have to be reduced and limited, especially when they make you feel really bad. Therefore, Dysfunctional Parent Modes and Vulnerable Child Modes are addressed separately, even though they often occur together.

In Dysfunctional Parent Mode people put excessive pressure on themselves, do not consider their own needs, think that their feelings are ridiculous, or devalue themselves for unjustified reasons.

Criticism or demands from your Dysfunctional Parent Modes can have different foci. It is important that you get to know all facets of your Dysfunctional Parent Mode. As remarked, one can differentiate between Demanding, Guilt-Inducing, and Punitive Parent Modes. Of course, it's sometimes a "mixed version," somewhere in between extreme demands and punitive messages. This is most often the case when several people devalued you in your childhood (e.g., parents, teachers, and classmates).

Demanding Parent Modes related to feelings of failure. Demanding Parent Modes are all about unrelenting standards in regard to the self. The main focus is on achievement in school, at university, or in your job. Strong Demanding Parent Modes in regard to shape and weight are common, too, especially in women. When the Mode's excessive demands cannot be fulfilled, people feel like failures.

Guilt-Inducing Parent Modes. "Guilt-inducing" means to make somebody else feel guilty. This Mode gives you the feeling that you are guilty of not fulfilling the expectations of your parents. Many people have difficulties setting limits in close relationships or expressing their own needs, because they feel that the needs of others are much more important. The most important messages are "you are responsible for making other people happy" and "you have to please and look after everyone." When you cannot live up to these demands you may feel guilty and depressed. This is why we speak of a Guilt-inducing Punitive Parent Mode.

Punitive Parent Mode. The Punitive Parent Mode is less about demands and more like an inner voice that simply denigrates and devalues the self. Often, the Punitive Parent Mode's messages are very broad and general. It may tell you that "you have always been like this," "you will never …," or "you are absolutely …," followed by negative attributes such as "stupid," "bad," or "ugly."

Some people suffer from "generalized" Dysfunctional Parent Modes. These Modes turn up in almost all situations and areas of their life. In other people these Modes may only be triggered in specific situations, such as those described in "More case examples of Dysfunctional Parent Modes."

The three different Dysfunctional Parent Modes are explained in more detail below.

Box 3.1: Typical Messages of Dysfunctional Parent Modes

Demanding Parent Modes with a focus on achievements and success:

- "You always have to be the best!"
- "If it's not perfect, it's worthless!"
- "If you're not skinny, you will never find a boyfriend!"

Guilt-inducing Parent Modes that cause feelings of guilt:

- "You have to take care of everyone!"
- "It's egoistic to put your needs in the center of attention!"
- "You have to be a perfect mother for your kids!"
- "You are bad if you do not put the needs of others above your own needs!"

Punitive Parent Modes:

- "You are a troublesome and difficult person."
- "When someone gets to know you, they will turn away from you!"
- "It would have been better if you had not been born!"

More Case Examples of Dysfunctional Parent Modes

1. **Generalized Punitive Parent Mode**. Annabelle was punished by the Magdalene sisters with food restriction and exposure when she gave her opinion. Moreover she had to do hard work as a punishment for even the smallest mistake. Physical pleasures (sexuality, cuddling, taking a long hot shower, etc.) were rejected, demonized, and sometimes even punished.

Today it is very difficult for Annabelle to take her own needs seriously and to allow herself any pleasure. Besides food, all physical pleasures, such as showering, sex, massages, or sunbathing, are "forbidden." When she feels that she has done something wrong (and she always feels as though she is doing things wrong), she feels awful and deserving of punishment. Annabelle is chronically depressed and very unstable due to these experiences. A long psychotherapy treatment will be necessary for her to overcome her Punitive Parent Mode, to learn to take good care of herself, and to become less strict with herself.

2. **A combination of Guilt-inducing and Demanding Parent Mode in specific situations**. Leah is a social worker – a job in which many people sacrifice themselves. Leah is usually able to keep within her limits. However, with young male clients it is somewhat different. She feels very responsible and protective for them and takes on duties and problems which her clients should actually deal with themselves.

    When Leah is on a workshop for prophylaxis in mental health she starts to think about this pattern. She is able to date it back to her childhood. Her younger brother was handicapped and she, as an older sister, helped to care for him from early on. When she looks closely at the feelings that her younger clients evoke they are very similar to her feeling of responsibility as an older sister towards her younger brother.

3.1   Demanding Parent Modes

Demanding Parent Modes with a focus on achievement and success push people to give their very best in everything. They may not rest until they are best at everything. When a student with a strong Demanding Parent Mode misses out just once on achieving the top score they may think of themselves as a failure, and may even think about changing their field of study. Demanding Parent Mode can lead to exhaustion and burnout, as you do not allow yourself any breaks but instead persist in seeking perfection and aiming for unachievable goals. People with this type of Parent Mode always put success, work, and discipline first. Joy, fun, and pleasure come a poor second.

Another typical Demanding Parent Mode can appear in the field of weight and body shape. Somebody with a strong Demanding Parent Mode will be very disciplined and controlled in regard to exercise and eating. Eating a dessert may be punished with excessive physical exertion. The biggest psychological problem related to this Mode is usually the feeling of failure.

It is often quite easy to pick out parents or parent figures with high standards in the life stories of people with strong Demanding Parent Modes. They may say about their childhood, "An A grade was good for my father, a B was OK, but he would always

Figure 3.1 Demanding Parent Mode

Case Example "Demanding Parent"

Lisa is 32 years old and mother of two little children. In her youth and during her time as a student she used to exercise a lot and was always very slim. She gained a few pounds after the birth of her children. In her everyday life there is rarely time for exercise, and so she has not shed the extra weight yet. Everyone thinks that Lisa still looks slim and fit, but she is dissatisfied with her shape and weight. She often resolves to start new diet and exercise schedules, but she can't keep them up due to stress and lack of time. She weighs herself every morning and when she has had a big dinner the scales sometimes show an extra pound. This makes her feel angry, frustrated, and desperate. The next day she will go jogging instead of having dinner.

---

disapprove of a B minus." In particular, lack of explicit praise will make people get into a perpetual race, always chasing higher achievements. They hope to reach a point when they are good enough and their parents are finally happy with them. From a child's perspective it is not possible to understand that it will never be good enough.

Many people with strong Demanding Parent Modes were engaged in competitive sports or played a musical instrument at a high standard in their childhood and adolescence. When we seek the origins of Demanding Parent Modes in therapy, we often uncover judo, gymnastics or track and field trainers, or piano teachers. "He was never satisfied, we always had to give everything in the training but nothing was ever good enough to satisfy him." After every achievement the child reached, there was always a new and higher target – it never came to an end. These dynamics are fueled by the competitive structure of the related systems. The child or adolescent has to climb up a ladder that extends and becomes steeper the higher they get. When a child is successful in sports or musical competitions, the next step is to compete on a higher level. This continues until they reach a level where success is no longer possible.

Case Example "Demanding Parent Mode in Sports"

Sebastian took part in competitive swimming as a teenager. At the local level he was a champion, which is why he started swimming in national competitions. Despite his extremely tough training he never did better than 6th or 7th. Sebastian learned from this to feel like a loser despite hard work and good results. His central memories regarding his career as a swimmer are not the successful local competitions, but his trainer's disappointment with the national results. Now, Sebastian is at college. When facing exams he experiences severe pressure and feels like a failure when he doesn't get excellent results. This feeling reminds him strongly of his situation as a competitive swimmer.

Box 3.2: Demanding Parent Mode or Healthy Ambition?

We are living in a world where you are expected to succeed – at work, in sports, or in your appearance. For many people this is accompanied by the experience of an "inner booster" pushing them to accomplish difficult goals. You may wonder about the difference between healthy ambition that drives you forward and a Demanding Parent Mode. The difference is how you feel about your ambitions, and whether your ambitions still allow you to fulfill important basic needs for rest, pleasure, attachment, etc. We would incline towards identifying Demanding Parent Mode if you experience difficulties such as sleep disturbance, intense rumination, binge eating or exhaustion related to stress and excessively high standards. Another sign of a Demanding Parent Mode is failure to participate in pleasant activities that fulfill the need for relaxation and fun (e.g., dancing, meeting friends, going to the movies). When you always "have to work" you are probably dealing with a Demanding Parent Mode. However, as long as you are feeling fine, you are not suffering from stress-related symptoms, and you manage to balance work and relaxation, you probably have healthy ambition driving you towards success.

You should be able to see from everything you've read so far that people who were the cause of a Demanding Parent Mode in a child probably had the best of intentions. However, the balance between praise and demands was out. It often happens that parents show affection and recognition through praise for achievements. Despite good intentions, this can lead to the child feeling loved only when he or she has accomplished something. Some children experience love and affection being taken away from them when they do not achieve good results, for instance when a mother shows disappointment and hardly talks to her son because he got a C grade at school. This is very distressing for children and can leave a permanent scar on the soul of a child. The child will do anything to avoid bad grades but will take no pleasure in accomplishing something – just strong disappointment and a feeling of being unloved when they fail.

It may be the case that parents, teachers, or other important people never explicitly asked for achievements from the child or adolescent. Instead they exemplify extreme commitment by never allowing themselves any time for relaxation and fun. Even if they reassure children that good grades are not everything in life, they display quite another example. Psychologists call this **"vicarious learning."**

Box 3.3: How does a Demanding Parent Mode Usually Develop?

- Parents or teachers emphasize the importance of grades and achievements very strongly.
- Parents deprive a child of love when they fail with something.
- A child is rewarded for achievements only.
- A child is active in a highly competitive system, for example, sports or music.

3.1.1   How can I detect my own Demanding Parent Mode?

The following statements help you to find out whether you have a strong Demanding Parent Mode or not.

- I don't allow myself to relax or to have fun until all the work is done.
- I am under permanent pressure to accomplish or achieve things.
- I try to never make a mistake. If I do, I punish myself.
- I know that there is a "good" and a "bad" way to do things. I try very hard to do everything in the right way. If I don't manage this, I am very critical of myself.

Worksheet 6, "My Demanding Parent Mode," will help you to recognize a Demanding Parent Mode and, if necessary, enable you to get more familiar with it. You may integrate the results in your Mode overview.

3.1.2   How can I detect a Demanding Parent Mode in other people?

When someone you interact with has a strong Demanding Parent Mode, you may get the impression that their perfectionism is really over the top. You may feel that they try way too hard and

Worksheet 6: My Demanding Parent Mode

My Demanding Parent Mode
My name for this Mode (e.g. Hurrier):
Messages of the Demanding Parent Mode:
1. How can I realize that my Demanding Parent Mode is present?
What is **triggering** my Demanding Parent Mode?
What **feelings** do I usually have in this Mode?
What **thoughts** tend to come up in this Mode?
What **memories** are associated/get triggered?
How does my **body** feel in this Mode?
How do I usually **behave** in this Mode?
2. Was my Demanding Parent Mode triggered by another Mode? By which one?
3. What are my actual **needs** when I am in the Demanding Parent Mode?
4. How does this Mode affect my feelings of safety?

take on much more responsibility than they should. Possibly, you think that their effort is often exaggerated. You may think, "Why do they have to do all that? That's not necessary! They could ask for help, nobody expects them to do everything by themselves" or "If they go on this way they will have a breakdown. It's too much, they need some rest." However, even if you tell them, they may not understand or accept your view, or they will not be able to relax anyway.

You almost certainly know people who always tend to over-stress themselves. Even when they feel exhausted they sign up for that extra task that nobody wants to do. Why can't they avoid these jobs just like everybody else? Probably a Demanding Parent Mode is involved.

Listen carefully to their answer when you confront them with their Demanding Parent Mode. If they are happy with your suggestion to get around the extra task, and act upon it, they probably do not suffer from a Demanding Parent Mode, but rather hadn't thought of a way to step aside from the task in the first place. But if they start explaining why they have to do more than anybody else you have probably encountered a Demanding Parent Mode.

3.2   Guilt-Inducing Parent Modes

In these Modes, people also set very high standards for themselves, but their demands focus on how someone should feel or behave in certain social situations. It is very common for people in such Modes to feel that they have to do everything for others and that they must not criticize anyone else. They feel that they always have to be nice and friendly, and responsible for the well-being of others; when they can't live up to this ideal they tend to feel guilty. People in social professions – physicians, psychotherapists, social workers, or nurses – often have this type of Parent Mode, at least to a degree.

Taking the role of your parent (parentification). The case of Violet is typical of the genesis of a Guilt-inducing Parent Mode.

Figure 3.2   Guilt-inducing Parent Mode

Case Example "Guilt-inducing Parent Mode"

Violet is a psychotherapist who is very popular with her clients. She is very empathic with other people, understands their problems, and can support, encourage, and cheer them up in a unique way. Nevertheless, she sometimes has difficulty setting boundaries both in her professional and her private life. She tries to take care of everything and everyone, even if she feels overstrained, and when she can't help someone she feels guilty and unloved.

Violet's mother suffered from depression. During depressive episodes she was very distant and dismissive, even towards her children. Violet always tried to cheer her up and to get a little smile. Because of that she still feels responsible for cheering everyone up. She feels as though she can't be loved until she makes everybody she deals with happy and satisfied.

People with a parent suffering from a mental disorder such as depression often develop a Guilt-inducing Parent Mode. This is because as children they felt personally responsible for their parent's mood and wellbeing. Other family members may feel overburdened with the disorder and cope with the situation by retreating from it. This may increase feelings of responsibility in the caring daughter, because she is, indeed, the only one who cares. In fact, this is a role reversal. Psychotherapists call this process "**parentification**": a child has had to take the role of an adult, especially its social and emotional parts, way too early. The child becomes the parent of its parent.

A similar situation occurs when parents separate and one of them uses the child as a "garbage can" by talking badly about the marriage or the former spouse. The child easily adopts the role of an advisor or negotiator, which again is not appropriate. When the child is not "successful" in this role, for example, failing to make the parents happy or save their relationship, he or she feels guilty and tries even harder. A child cannot understand that this function is inappropriate and outside its limits. Instead they may simply take it as normal and internalize the role as a Demanding Parent Mode for the rest of their life.

Vicarious learning. Learning from somebody else (i.e., a role model) can also lead to the acquisition of an emotionally Demanding Parent Mode. People with a strong Mode of this type have often experienced a situation in their childhood where all the family members had to adjust their life and needs to the needs of one person, such as a physically or mentally ill sibling or parent.

Or everybody had to pretend to father/grandfather/grandmother that they were happy and satisfied and loved them deeply. You had to play this role, no matter what your true feelings were. In such cases, everyone in the family circle is obliged to show emotions, attention, affection, or joy which they do not actually feel. Later in life they may feel guilty when they openly display disapproval.

Case Example "Emotionally Demanding Parent Mode"

Anna is a nurse. She is very popular, always calm and in a good mood. Nevertheless, she is aware that patients with bossy behaviors and who made heavy demands are extremely distressing to her. When she deals with these patients she becomes hectic and feels bad when they are not satisfied.

They resemble Anna's father. Life was always quite pleasant for Anna's family when their father was absent. But when he came home after work, the whole family had to try hard to keep his mood up, to avoid him getting irritated and bossy. Nobody ever explicitly advised Anna to behave in a certain way, but from her early childhood she learned to follow her mother's example.

In extreme cases it may even be dangerous not to play a certain role. Daughters of alcoholic fathers, for example, often came to realize that their fathers were irritable, incalculable, or even violent when they were drunk. Sometimes, the mother stayed in the marriage despite dangerous violence from the father. She always reacted submissively in order to calm him down. Children in such family constellations often experience anxiety and threat when they try to express their needs in a relationship or to criticize their partner later in life, even if there is no longer a real reason to worry.

Box 3.4: Typical Biographical Situations for the Genesis of an Emotionally Demanding or Guilt-inducing Parent Mode

- **Parentification:** Parents were emotionally unstable and the child learned to be responsible for the wellbeing of others from early on.
- **Vicarious learning:** A child learned from other family members to play a certain role in order to please somebody.
- A (physically or psychologically) violent family member could be calmed down when everybody pleased them.

3.2.1   How can I detect Guilt-inducing Parent Modes?

With the help of the following statements you can check whether you have a Guilt-inducing Parent Mode:

- I try very hard to make it right for everyone and to avoid conflicts, arguments, or rejection from others.
- I am a bad person if I get angry at others.
- I force myself to take more responsibility than most other people.

You can find questions with regard to your Guilt-inducing Parent Mode in Worksheet 7. You may add this information to your Mode overview. In your everyday life you can recognize this Mode by the feelings of pressure and guilt that make it really hard to show your needs, even if it would actually be completely justified.

With regard to Guilt-inducing Parent Modes in others, you may suspect this Mode if you feel that someone should not put so much effort into making it right for everyone else. You may feel that they should pursue their own needs more strongly. But if, when you tell

Worksheet 7: My Guilt-inducing Parent Mode

My Guilt-inducing Parent Mode
My name for this Mode (e.g. Mother Therese):
Messages of the Guilt-inducing Parent Mode:
1. How can I realize that my Guilt-inducing Parent Mode is present?
What **triggering** my Guilt-inducing Parent Mode?
What **feelings** do I usually have in this Mode?
What **thoughts** tend to come up in this Mode?
What **memories** are associated/get triggered?
How does my **body** feel in this Mode?
How do I usually **behave** in this Mode?
2. Was my Guilt-Inducing Parent Mode triggered by another Mode? By which one?
3. What are my actual **needs** when I am in the Guilt-inducing Parent Mode?
4. How does this Mode affect my feelings of safety?

them, they will not accept it, even if they would like to, then you are justified in assuming there is a Guilt-inducing Parent Mode.

3.3 Punitive Parent Mode

In the Punitive Parent Mode people devalue, denigrate or even hate themselves. In their childhood, these people often experienced emotional, physical, or sexual abuse. An example would be a girl who was teased by her classmates because of her big breasts. It is quite likely that this woman will feel ashamed of her breasts, or even of her whole body, for the rest of her life. Or think of a boy who was cruelly punished for the slightest mistakes. Later in his life he will probably feel as if he deserves to be punished when he slips up.

There are different types of abuse that can result in a Punitive Parent Mode. Some people even experience several types of abuse simultaneously.

Figure 3.3 Punitive Parent Mode

Sexual abuse. This is probably the best-known type of abuse. In some cases the perpetrator is the father or stepfather. However, other people can be perpetrators, such as neighbors or people in positions of trust like leaders of youth organizations, priests, or sports trainers. Sexual abuse leads to a Punitive Parent Mode for several reasons. Sexually abused children are often ashamed of what has happened even though they are not to blame. In addition, perpetrators often make the children feel that it is their fault. Abused children often feel that they deserve no better treatment – in a way, the assault is proof that they are obviously bad.

Physical abuse. Physically abused children are battered or physically harmed in other ways. Sometimes the perpetrator basically has a bad temper and is very impulsive. In other cases, physical abuse seems to be rather sadistic, meaning that the perpetrator finds pleasure in abusing the child. This leads most often to severe psychological scars and to strong Punitive Parent Modes. Physical abuse can also happen between classmates or peers, with terrible psychological consequences for the victim.

Emotional abuse. This means that children are harmed psychologically by their parents or others. Emotionally abusive parents may tell their child that it is guilty, and responsible for their problems; that they would be happier if the child had not been born. They may leave the house announcing suicide, etc. Note that these examples are rather extreme – emotional abuse can also be more subtle and inconspicuous.

Neglect. When neglected children feel that they are not worthy of good care they will probably internalize this as a strong Punitive Parent Mode. Neglect can be a failure to care for a child's basic physical needs, such as food, clothing, warmth, etc. However, emotional needs can also be neglected, for example when a parent is insensitive to a child, does not support it in dealing with problems at school or with friends, leaves the child alone without saying when they will be coming back, etc.

Other severe punishments. Some people experience very cruel punishment in their childhood. Examples are being locked outside the house naked, being excluded from meals, or being locked away in a dark cellar. Such experiences leave deep scars and most likely will only be overcome with professional psychotherapy.

Mobbing. Mobbing between classmates or peers can be an extreme and long-lasting type of abuse. People often report mobbing situations that went on for years. Mobbing by classmates is disastrous, because you have to spend almost every day for many years with the same people. Uncovering the mobbing situation might make the perpetrators feel offended and can even worsen the situation for the victim! This constellation induces strong helplessness and pressure to surrender.

Case Examples "Punitive Parent Mode"

1. Julia is a 28-year-old psychotherapy patient with borderline personality disorder. She cannot manage to live a normal life and pursue goals like other people. When a small problem or conflict comes up, Julia injures herself and retreats completely. As a child she was severely abused by her grandfather over many years. Although the family guessed what was going on, nobody took action and Julia was sent to her grandparents over and over again. Today she hates herself, and in particular her body. She feels that she deserves bad treatment. She ignores her own needs, and will certainly not talk about them. She punishes herself with self-injury when the feeling of self-hatred overwhelms her.
2. Patricia cannot stand herself and hardly allows herself any food. Eating provokes feelings of disgust in her. She grew up in a foster family with a sadistic foster mother, who was presumably overstrained with her foster children and often accused Patricia of stealing food. As a punishment she was sent to bed without dinner and locked in her room. Patricia's foster mother was wrong to

accuse Julia most of the time but punished her cruelly nevertheless.

3.   Danny has an antisocial personality disorder. His father battered him for years. Even if he did not do anything wrong he was battered and locked in his room without food and water. His father told him that he was a bad person and no good for anything. Danny lived on the streets and became involved with a criminal youth gang. He used cocaine, alcohol, and amphetamines. He thought, "If they say that I'm bad, I'll prove they're right." Sometimes he's used drugs in an attempt to destroy himself. He is convinced that he is actually not worthy of living.

Punitive Parent Modes can have different "messages." They are almost always related to being unlovable. Moreover, these messages can comprehend shame and disgust in regard to the self, for example, addressing needs that had been punished in childhood. People with a strong Punitive Parent Mode can rarely see that their needs and rights are important.

3.3.1   *How can I detect a Punitive Parent Mode in myself?*

The following statements help you to check whether you suffer from a Punitive Parent Mode:

- I am not allowed to do pleasant things like other people because I am bad.
- I deserve punishment.
- I have the urge to punish and hurt myself (e.g., cutting myself).
- I cannot forgive myself.

If you hate yourself most of the time; feel ashamed of yourself, your feelings and needs; or think that you cannot expect anyone to spend time with you, you are certainly suffering from a Punitive Parent Mode. You can hardly believe that anyone likes you or that you are important to anybody. In Worksheet 8 you will find questions to ask

Worksheet 8: My Punitive Parent Mode

My Punitive Parent Mode
My name for this Mode (e.g. Inquisitor):
Messages of the Punitive Parent Mode:
1. How can I realize that my Punitive Parent Mode is present?
What is **triggering** my Punitive Parent Mode?
What **feelings** do I usually have in this Mode?
What **thoughts** tend to come up in this Mode?
What **memories** are associated/get triggered?
How does my **body** feel in this Mode?
How do I usually **behave** in this Mode?
2. Was my Demanding Parent Mode triggered by another Mode (e.g. Vulnerable Child) By which one?
3. What are my actual **needs** when I am in the Punitive Parent Mode?
4. How does this Mode affect my feelings of safety?

yourself about your Punitive Parent Mode. You may add this information in the Mode overview.

3.3.2   How can I detect a Punitive Parent Mode in others?

An important sign of a Punitive Parent Mode in somebody else is that positive messages do not seem to reach them. The person does not value himself or herself no matter how hard you try to convince them that a little mistake is not important or that they are loved and precious.

The person in question may ask all the time if you can still stand being around them. Or they emphasize over and over again that they are stupid and annoying. Maybe you feel desperate around this person because your view of them is completely different. You might even get angry after a while because you feel that all your effort to express sympathy and interest in the other person is not reaching them. The Punitive Parent Mode stands like a wall between the two of you.

Case Example "Punitive Parent Mode"

Charlotte has a strong Punitive Parent Mode. As a child she was physically abused and was left with the feeling of being absolutely worthless. Today, Charlotte is a lovable woman who has some loyal and reliable friends. Her friend Christine has similar problems, although less severe. Christine sometimes tries to question Charlotte's punitive self-perception. She suggests that Charlotte sees things from a different perspective to make her realize how good she is. However, Charlotte hardly reacts to such efforts from her friend. She seems to hear the words but the information does not "stick." Christine gets frustrated by her reaction and resolves to let Charlotte stay "on her own planet" the next time, although she feels so sorry for her.

You may have noticed that in Punitive Parent Modes a vicious circle can be triggered, as with the Vulnerable Child Mode. People with a strong Punitive Parent Mode feel that they do not have the same rights as other people. Close friends will probably have a completely different opinion on that. They care about the other person's needs and would be happy to see them enforce their rights. Nevertheless, people with a strong Punitive Parent Mode seem to be "deaf" to such encouragement. Because of their self-hatred, they might even repel people who want the best for them. This urge to punish the self can even lead to devaluation of others – just because they are interested in oneself!

3.4   Summary

Dysfunctional Parent Modes are a kind of negative inner voice telling you over and over again that you are bad or worthless and that you will never be accepted or loved by others.

The name "Dysfunctional Parent Mode" does not mean that your parents were bad or that your parents gave you these negative messages. Sometimes some parts of the parents' behavior may have been damaging, but not everything they did. Within families it might be people other than the parents (such as grandparents or siblings) who make a child feel bad or insufficient. Children are often bullied and excluded by their classmates, which can cause lifelong feelings of rejection.

We distinguish three Dysfunctional Parent Modes. The *Demanding Parent Mode* is developed when parents or teachers focus on accomplishments and success, and only show affection and recognition through praise for achievement; it is never good enough. The *Guilt-inducing Parent Mode* arises from parents who have (psychological) problems themselves and make their child responsible for their wellbeing or marital problems. The child has to take the role of an adult, especially its social and emotional parts, far too early in life. The *Punitive Parent Mode* is caused by emotional, physical, or sexual abuse by parents or other caregivers.

You can put the information about Dysfunctional Parent Modes in your personal Mode overview.

It is not always easy to detect your Parent Modes. If you have a Spoilt or Undisciplined Child Mode it is especially difficult to find out whether you also have a Dysfunctional Parent Mode. Maybe you do not have a self-critical inner voice at all because your parents put too little pressure on you and did not give you healthy limitations. If your parents were ill or had a lot of problems you still only feel sorry for them and don't feel they did anything wrong.

In the next chapters you can detect how you "survived" the negative messages of your parents and developed different possibilities for dealing with difficult emotional experiences. The ways you dealt with difficult or threatening situations are called "coping styles."

4

Coping Modes

In the previous chapters dealing with Dysfunctional Child and Parent Modes we explained how people develop hurtful inner elements when they experience abuse or rejection during childhood and adolescence. Everyone has some experience of such Child and Parent Modes, even if only to a limited extent. Some people manage to feel well despite such experiences because these dysfunctional elements are not very strong or tend to be triggered only rarely. However, people who are afflicted with strong Modes of these types will run into emotional problems over and over again.

Whether you experience these Modes frequently or rarely you'll be aware that human beings differ in their ability to deal with difficult emotional experiences. Many psychologists call the processes by which people address these difficulties "coping styles." A coping style is kind of psychological survival strategy to deal with threatening emotions and experiences. Coping styles differ from person to person: just like emotions, coping styles are often influenced by childhood experiences. The intensity of Coping Modes most often depends on the strength of the related Dysfunctional Child and Parent Modes.

Breaking Negative Thinking Patterns: A Schema Therapy Self-Help and Support Book,
First Edition. Gitta Jacob, Hannie van Genderen and Laura Seebauer.
© 2011 Beltz Psychologie in der Verlagsgruppe
Beltz • Weinheim Basel. Published 2015 by John Wiley & Sons, Ltd.

Three Coping Modes. In general, therapists differentiate between the following three Coping Modes, although they often overlap:

- **Surrendering**. In this coping style you surrender to the Punitive, Critical or Guilt-inducing Parent Mode and start thinking negatively about yourself, and feeling bad.
- **Avoidance**. In this coping style you avoid emotions and problems and so you don't have to be confronted with them.
- **Overcompensation**. In this coping style you act in the opposite way to the feelings and demands of your Dysfunctional Parent Modes. You may display excessive self-confidence or seek to control other people in order to avoid feelings of insecurity or helplessness.

In this chapter you will learn more about these three coping styles. As a first step we will give you an overview on how to distinguish them.

Figure 4.1   Surrendering

Surrendering. We talk about surrendering when a person behaves as if the messages from their Dysfunctional Parent and Child Modes are absolutely true. They do not see how to "escape" from difficult situations in a healthy way. So they start feeling bad, sad, miserable or guilty, or even mad at themselves. When they are asked to express their own needs, they may feel helpless and avoid doing so.

Case Examples "Surrendering"

1. As a child, Holly experienced sexual abuse by her grandfather. Her grandmother was aware of the abuse, but did not dare to raise her voice against her husband. Later in life, Holly gives in to the sexual desires of any man who wants her. When a man wants to find out what she actually wants herself, she cannot say and feels horribly insecure.

2. Joshua has a strong Guilt-inducing Parent Mode. It has its origin in his depressed mother, who frequently asked him for support when he was a child. Nowadays, Joshua is a social worker who sacrifices himself for his clients and often overburdens himself. He is always willing to care about their problems even when his working hours are over and even though his boss has asked him to set stricter limits in his dealings with clients. In his private life he does everything to make his girlfriend happy and completely forgets to take care of himself. When his girlfriend wants to do something nice for him, he can hardly feel his own inner needs.

3. Nora has a strong demanding parent side forcing her to do everything perfectly. She works day and night. If she takes even a short rest she always feels the pressure to start doing something useful. She is perpetually afraid of being a failure. She surrenders to her achievement-oriented demanding parent side.

Avoidance. People often avoid distressing emotions related to Dysfunctional Child or Parent Modes by avoiding certain situations or by consuming sedating substances like alcohol or benzodiazepine. We talk about someone employing an avoidant style of coping when they act to put a distance between themselves and a difficult emotional experience. Note that we only talk of a Coping Mode when the reaction is *dysfunctional*, i.e. by showing this reaction the person fails to care for their own needs or fulfill their usual obligations.

Avoidant patterns can be related to very different actions, including avoidant behavior in a narrow sense (e.g. social retreat or not attending work), use of emotionally numbing substances (alcohol, cannabis, benzos, etc.), or other distracting behaviors (e.g., eating to cope with feelings; excessive consumption of TV or video games). In people with severe mental disorders, different symptoms can be related to Avoidant Coping. For instance, starving oneself (anorectic symptoms) reduces emotional experiences; some patients with borderline personality disorder injure themselves to escape strong negative emotions, etc.

Overcompensation. Overcompensation means that someone confronts a deficit with an excess. We talk about an overcompensating coping style when someone behaves as if the opposite of their Vulnerable Child and Dysfunctional Parent Modes' messages were true. For example, someone who is feeling inferior

Figure 4.2   Avoidance

Case Examples "Avoidance"

1. Isabella has a strong Punitive Parent Mode telling her that nobody likes her and that she is ugly. Since she was a little child she has been teased about her knock-knees and her acne. Her family used to compare her unfavorably to her pretty sister. As a result she feels ashamed when she is around other people. She avoids these feelings mainly by social retreat (avoidant behavior). When she does go out, she usually drinks much more alcohol than she actually wants, probably because when she is drunk she feels less ashamed and anxious.

2. Jake was a very good high school student. His family was strongly oriented towards achievement and he developed a strong Demanding Parent Mode. At university he suddenly found himself as merely one of many talented students, struggling with the same difficulties as everybody else. He can no longer always satisfy his Demanding Parent Mode by being the best. As time goes by he draws back from the university. Instead he spends his time playing "World of Warcraft" and other video games, surfing the Internet, and watching TV. All these can be considered avoidant behaviors to escape his feelings of failure.

3. Catherine has a strong Guilt-inducing Parent Mode telling her that she is responsible for everything and has to support everybody. She has often helped her neighbor with various issues. Though Catherine likes to help her, the neighbor, who is a very lonely woman, clings to Catherine. She'd love to talk for several hours a day, which is way too much… Catherine, however, is simply unable to set limits to the neighbor's demands. Instead, she has taken to looking through the spyhole in her door to check whether the "coast is clear" – her neighbor is not around – before leaving the apartment. Catherine knows that she should set clearer limits to her neighbor's excessive demands. However, the pressure of her Guilt-inducing Parent Mode is too strong, so she avoids encounters with the woman.

to others might overcompensate by behaving excessively self-confidently or even arrogantly. Or a man who feels insecure with women starts behaving like a macho. Someone who feels helpless may try to be very controlling with others.

Just like avoidance, overcompensation can take many forms. What they all have in common is that the overcompensating person seeks to control and dominate the situation. Everyone else gets the feeling that it's impossible to go against the wishes and opinions of the overcompensating person.

Figure 4.3   Overcompensation

Case Examples "Overcompensation"

1. Ruby experienced physical and sexual violence when she was a child. Nowadays, when somebody merely holds another opinion than herself, she tends to feel threatened and helpless. She overcompensates for these feelings with a very aggressive set of behaviors: she gets loud and screams at others, trying to intimidate them. She does this even when it is completely inappropriate. She feels that only aggressive behavior will enable her to get her needs met.

2. Carl is a small, plump, rather unattractive man who grew up in a rich family of entrepreneurs. However, the family company went into bankruptcy some years ago, so his wealth is gone. He's always felt inferior because of his unattractive appearance. This feeling has been enhanced by the loss of his money. He compensates for his feelings of inferiority by behaving in an extremely self-confident and macho way. Most other people can see straight away that he actually feels inferior and is compensating by showing off.

3. Benjamin was forced by his father to stay in his room for hours to do his homework. He started to resist his father and they frequently had arguments. Eventually, he stopped doing his homework, took to missing classes, and started using cannabis and cocaine – later, even heroin. He was kicked out of school. His father became very frustrated and disappointed in him. Benjamin didn't finish his education and became an addict.

He used drugs not only to feel better but actually to resist his father's demands. Using drugs has given him the feeling that he controls his father by doing the opposite of what his father actually wants. He has developed a narcissistic personality disorder.

Note that it is important for all of us to be able to cope with negative emotions when they overwhelm us. Coping strategies help us to survive difficult emotions and situations. Psychoanalysts call coping styles "defense mechanisms" and assume that every healthy individual needs them. Thus, emotional avoidance can be useful from time to time. Think of conflicts which can never come to a good solution – for example an annoying neighbor whose cats frequently foul your lawn. You will come across an annoying neighbor no matter where you live, so moving might not be the solution... W hat you should rather try to do is avoid angry feelings, because you may not be able to come to a solution and the issue is actually not so very important to you. You might as well just invest in a shovel and some cat repellent, and ignore your neighbor.

A coping style becomes a Dysfunctional Coping Mode when it stands in the way of you getting your needs met. For example if you try to avoid all types of conflict – not only with your annoying neighbor, but also with your significant others, such as your friends or your partner – you will not be able to address your own needs in your interactions with these important people, and in the long run the relationships will not develop in the way you need them to.

Maybe you have already picked up a feeling for your typical coping style(s) from your reading of the case examples. It is fairly normal for a person to use different coping styles in different situations. Someone with a strong Guilt-inducing Parent Mode, for example, may cope for a long time by surrendering and trying to care for everyone's needs. However, when this strategy becomes too much to bear they might switch to coping by avoiding and start to shun social situations. Alternatively, they might activate an overcompensating coping style and push back harshly on people who make even the smallest demand.

Coping patterns develop differently in childhood and adolescence. Usually, Coping Modes develop unconsciously to "survive" difficult situations. A particular coping style was probably the best way to protect yourself from difficulties, rejection or threat, when you were a child or adolescent. It was only later in your life that it became a Dysfunctional Mode. We often learn Coping Modes from role models: we observe how another person reacts to problematic situations or feelings. Think of a family with a verbally abusive father and a mother who does not set limits and does not protect her children, but instead surrenders to the father. These children in their turn have a high risk of developing a surrendering coping style in the face of aggression.

As always, different pathways may act together in the development of Coping Modes. When a child feels threatened by its father and observes its mother surrendering, it sees a surrendering role model. This will make the child feel even less safe, since the mother does not offer protection. The feeling of being exposed to danger increases the child's motivation to develop Coping Modes of its own.

4.1   Compliant Surrender Mode

When someone is in a Surrendering Coping Mode they care about the needs of others and not at all about their own. They allow others to treat them badly. They do things they actually do not want to do because others want or demand it – even though from an objective point of view they are not obliged to do so. They accede to the wishes of others in private, sexual, or other relationships, even though their own wishes are different.

Often, these people sense that they are actually not happy or satisfied with the way that they behave. But sometime they may actually use additional strategies associated with Avoidant Coping to keep the Surrender Mode going. For example a woman surrendering in sexual relationships may drink alcohol because getting drunk before sex is easier for her than setting a healthy limit, or saying "No."

Now, take a moment to think about the times that you give in to the demands of others, even if they are not congruent with your own needs and feelings. Do you experience situations in which you do things that you actually don't want to do and aren't obliged to do? What feelings drive you in these situations? What are you afraid of that stops you setting limits? Do you have an idea about the origin of this behavior? When and why you did develop this Mode?

You may add your own examples to Worksheet 9, "My Surrendering Coping Mode." It can help you to detect pros and cons of your surrendering and develop ideas for alternative behaviors.

Sometimes, so-called dependent relationship patterns are linked to the Compliant Surrender Coping Mode. People with strong interpersonal dependency will not take responsibility for their own life. Instead, they always need someone to take care of them and make decisions for them. Only then do they feel safe. Interpersonal dependency is linked with surrendering coping, since dependent people are willing to give up a lot to make sure that they have someone to take responsibility for them.

4.1.1   How can I detect a Compliant Surrender Coping Mode in myself?

The following statements will help you to estimate how strong your surrender patterns are:

- In case of trouble or difficulty, I think: "You see, this has to happen to me again."
- In case of difficulty I tend to give up.
- If others treat me badly I let it happen.
- I let others determine my life.
- I let others get their way instead enforcing my own interests.

An easy way to identify surrendering behavior is to ask yourself whether you do things that you actually either don't *want* or don't *have* to do. No one likes doing their taxes, but completing your tax return is not surrendering behavior because although you may not *want* to do it you simply *have* to do it. But you *should* think about your Surrendering Coping Mode if it's always you

Worksheet 9: My Surrendering Coping Mode

My Surrendering Coping Mode			
	Origin of my coping style	*Positive and negative consequences of my coping behavior*	*How do others react in similar situations?*
1. Personal example			
2. Personal example			

Worksheet 9a: Example of a "Surrender" Worksheet

My Surrendering Coping Mode

	Origin of my coping style	Positive and negative consequences of my coping behavior	How do others react in similar situations?
My manager told me to revise my text. My Demanding Parent Mode is triggered. Coping Mode: working on my text till late in the evening to make it perfect.	When my father was criticized he always tried to please everyone. If I was treated unfairly at school he always told me to work harder. He never supported me.	NEGATIVE: I always work too long. POSITIVE: My manager is very happy with me. NEGATIVE: I have conflicts with my wife. NEGATIVE: My manager increases his demands.	Someone else would listen to the comments and then consider whether they are justified. Then he would decide how much time is needed and whether this is reasonable.
My partner doesn't want to help with the housekeeping. Coping Mode: I do everything by myself and tell myself that he is too busy with his work. I make my job less important.	My mother did all the housekeeping and didn't have a job. My father didn't have to learn how to do the housekeeping.	POSITIVE: No conflicts with my partner. POSITIVE: The housekeeping is exactly how I want it. NEGATIVE: I do not have enough time for pleasant things. NEGATIVE: I have a lot of stress. NEGATIVE: I feel abused.	My best friend had the same problem with her husband. She confronted him and they made a plan how to share the housekeeping.

Box 4.1: Interpersonal Dependency

Interpersonal dependency indicates that you are psychologically over-dependent on other people, i.e. you cling to them and feel that you could not survive without them (even though, objectively, this is not the case). People in dependent relationships usually behave submissively. In extreme cases they rarely take decisions, leaving this up their partner. Typically, they feel that they can't live on their own. Therefore they tend to accept things – they don't want to put the relationship at risk.

Dependency is often a feature of intimate relationships. Some people with dependent patterns may constantly search for "helpers" to direct and support them (e.g. medical doctors, psychotherapists, or other care-givers). Dependency might also be a problem in other private relationships with friends or relatives. The following features are typical for dependency (American Psychiatric Association, 2000).

- Dependent people look for a lot of advice and reassurance before coming to everyday decisions.
- They depend on others for the organization of important areas in their lives, such as financial issues, education of children, or planning their daily routine.
- It's difficult for them to answer back to someone, even if the other person is wrong.
- It's also difficult for them to try out new things if there's no one available to assist them.
- They often accept annoying responsibilities in order to obtain or retain support and affection from others.
- They usually feel uncomfortable when they are alone.
- When an important relationship ends, they need someone else very quickly.
- They're afraid of being abandoned and on their own.

These patterns have many long-term disadvantages and high "costs." However, if you're in a dependent pattern you'll find there are several (mainly short-term) advantages: you can easily avoid responsibility if you do not come to your own decisions. Negative consequences of a decision are not "your fault." When you always avoid responsibility you're taking an easy way of avoiding criticism.

Furthermore, people with dependent patterns can force close attachment on to others. If you behave in a submissive and devoted way, the other person may feel that they can never leave. Thus the most important need, for attachment and affiliation, will be fulfilled for the dependent person – although the cost is that many other important needs are not met.

Nevertheless, it's not promising in the long run to attach yourself to others by dependent patterns. It may be possible to override relationship problems by dependent behavior for a while, but eventually there will be problems if one person takes responsibility for everything in a relationship, and if needs and boundaries are not openly discussed.

If you think you have dependent patterns it's probably hard to admit it and it will be unpleasant to take an objective look at your behavior. Nevertheless, a clear and realistic perspective on your dependent behavior is crucial if you want to change it. Always keep in mind that in the long run a pattern change will pay off for you – you have the chance to live *your* life…! However, it is always very hard to make pattern changes that have strong short-term consequences… so you'd better be really sure about what you do and don't want.

who takes over annoying voluntary jobs in your relationship, in the kindergarten etc. You should try to be objective here – mostly people tend to overestimate their own contributions (**balance in social relationships**). However if you tend to give in to sexual practices you really don't like, or if you go to the movies with your partner each week although you'd prefer to exercise, it might be about surrendering.

Take a moment to reflect how you would feel if you didn't take the assignment, or if you rejected your partner's wishes and instead enforced some of your own interests. If the idea of being less compliant evokes strong anxiety (Vulnerable Child Mode) or a guilty conscience (Dysfunctional Parent Mode), you probably have a Compliant Surrender Mode.

You can often work these things out by thinking about a good friend. How would you feel if a good friend were to act in such a surrendering way? It's usually easier for us to detect a dysfunctional mode in others than in ourselves.

When someone finally tries to reduce their submissive behavior other people may react in irritation. In other words, fears of being criticized and rejected might really be justified at first! If you are a surrendering type, you have to realize that you are in a vicious circle (surrendering leads to more demands from your environment which leads to surrendering). You have to break this circle in order to reduce your Compliant Surrender Mode.

Case Examples: Compliant Surrender or Not?

1. Anna is a mother of three children and works part time. Her husband has a full-time job with lots of work even at night and at weekends. She often feels that she has to take care of everything. The children are always sick or in need of extra help – homework, exercise, piano lessons… She has already hired a cleaning woman but still the daily demands never end…

    Does Anna suffer from a Compliant Surrender Coping Mode? Probably not! Note that Anna actively hired someone to help her – obviously she is able to ask for support. She does not feel that everything is her duty. Moreover, having children and working at the same time is simply stressful for everybody. The never-ending to-do list is, unfortunately, normal. Just look at other working moms …

2. Elsie works part-time and has an 11-year-old child. Like all working moms she always has a lot to do. Recently she noticed that she seems to be a magnet for extra assignments nobody likes. She used to serve as parent associate in her sons' kindergarten and in primary school. She was absolutely determined not to catch this job when her son started high school – and now she's got it again! She just couldn't stand the pressure and the rising feelings of guilt and responsibility when nobody else was willing to take the job… Apart from that she frequently assists her mother with her household and goes shopping for her groceries – despite her childless sister living much closer to her mother's house. Elsie often feels angry at her sister, but never addresses this issue with her mother.

    Does Elsie have a Compliant Surrender Mode? Most likely, yes! She takes on more responsibilities than others although she doesn't want them. She does so because if she doesn't do it she feels guilty and responsible. Other people don't seem to have the same feelings in the same situations.

3. Summer grew up with a violent, alcoholic father who used to beat her severely. Her current partner is an alcoholic and very violent, too. He has been to prison for assault. When he demands something from her she immediately follows his command. Often she feels disgusted by his sexual contact but she gives in because she fears that he might get aggressive.

    Does Summer show signs of a Compliant Surrender Mode? Absolutely! Moreover, it's important to note that Summer lives in a dangerous situation. To change that it's not recommended (and probably too dangerous) for her to express her needs towards her partner–if anything he would react with more violence! Instead, Summer needs to protect herself, for example by escaping to a shelter for battered women.

4.1.2 How can I detect a Compliant Surrender Mode in others?

It's a clear sign of surrendering when one of the partners in a close relationship anticipates the other's every wish. In the short run this might be very pleasant for the spoilt one, but in the long run it might become annoying when the partner is permanently submissive. You may want to know what your partner really likes, not be "pampered" all the time.

If you observe submissive behavior in other relationships you may feel that one partner is "dancing to the other partner's tune." You might get really annoyed and think: "Why is she willing to let anything happen to her? She should stand up for herself." You may come to understand how a submissive pattern developed when you learn more about a person's history.

When people react submissively they often fall into relationships with others who find this kind of behavior convenient. The social environment becomes accustomed to one individual always taking the unpleasant assignments...

4.2 Avoidant Coping Mode

The key feature of this Coping Mode is that people avoid things that they find difficult. "Difficult things" might be performance requirements, conflicts with others, social contact (in general or with particular people), but also negative emotions or thinking about oneself and one's problems.

There is a huge range of things you can do to avoid something. In a narrow sense, avoidance occurs when you simply avoid doing certain things – you don't attend certain situations, you avoid difficult topics in discussions, etc. But other behaviors, such as excessive distraction, can also count as avoidance, for instance when someone watches TV, plays computer games, or surfs the Internet nonstop instead of caring about their "real world" tasks. Some of these activities are highly stimulating, like watching porn movies or playing first-person shooter Internet games. Moreover, consumption of drugs such as alcohol, cannabis, or tranquilizers (often benzodiazepines) can serve the purpose of avoidance. Some people tend to grumble or moan about everything; however, you get the impression that they actually feel quite content within their grumbling Mode. If you try to interrupt them, they stick to their never-ending complaints rather than discussing solutions. Such behavior can sometimes be classified as avoidance.

Some examples of behaviors associated with Avoidant Coping Mode are listed in Box 4.2.

Box 4.2: Typical Avoidant Behavior Patterns

- **Avoidance in a narrow sense**. Staying away from difficult situations, avoiding particular tasks.
- **Distraction.** Computer games, excessive Internet use, watching movies, loud music, non-stop working, excessive participation in sports.
- **Stimulation.** Overeating, watching porn, gambling, risky sports.
- **Weakening perception**. Unpleasant feelings are avoided by drinking alcohol or using drugs.
- **Moaning and grumbling.** Monotonous, stereotyped moaning, grumbling, complaining; blaming others for everything. Frequently these people do not really seem to suffer or to be really angry. It's more that their usual habit is to grumble and complain.
- **Low expectations.** It's another form of avoidance not to set yourself any goals – then you don't feel disappointed by encountering problems reaching them...

Case Examples

1. Harry is a student in economics. He suffers from high social anxiety. He had been bullied at school because of his small, plump figure, and university is a tough place for him as it often reminds him of his high school experiences. Although he succeeded in losing weight and eventually reached an average height, at this stage he can't get rid of his feelings of inferiority.

   Harry tends to avoid difficult situations. He repeatedly fails to register for exams because he is anxious not to fail. He avoids contact with his fellow students by always sitting close to the door in the lecture hall – thus he does not have to talk to others. When he is invited to a party, he usually agrees to come but never shows up. Instead he spends his nights watching TV and playing Internet games.

2. Caitlin is afraid of other people. Her father was an alcoholic who used to beat her mother. As a result she feels easily threatened by other people even without any reason. Today she works as a sales clerk in a toy store. Her customers are sometimes quite demanding – then she feels under pressure and "not good enough." Some years ago she discovered that alcohol melted away her fears. That is why she now always has a bottle of wine close to hand. A glass sipped throughout the morning helps her to shut off emotional distress. She has a sense that, like her father, she might have a problem with alcohol, but most of the time she can suppress that idea.

3. When 14-year-old Lydia is sad she just needs something to eat. When she is heartsick or stressed at school she nibbles a bar of chocolate or a bag of candy. She knows that she should not, but it just happens automatically – she feels driven towards candy. It somehow makes her feel better, or at least less sad and alone.

4.2.1   How can I detect Avoidant Coping Mode in myself?

The following statements will help you to estimate whether you tend to have behavior patterns that indicate Avoidance Coping Mode, and how strong they are.

- I would rather not have intimate friendships or relationships.
- I prefer to avoid confrontation.
- It is best to switch of your feelings as much as possible.
- I like to keep it superficial.

It definitely requires some self-critical reflection to admit avoidance. It's often the case that you know better and you see how constantly playing video games, eating, avoiding etc. is not helpful.

However, sometimes it's quite difficult to detect your own avoidance, as it is so multi-faceted. It is avoiding when you don't do things that would be good or necessary, but it can also be avoidance to engage excessively with details or to distract yourself instead of attending to your real tasks (often called "displacement"). If you have habits that you actually dislike –perhaps drinking too much or eating too much candy, check if they are related to avoidance. Maybe you drink alcohol when you actually feel anxious and insecure? Or maybe you devour candy when you are dissatisfied or feel empty? Eating can soothe and comfort you and distract you from negative feelings. This could be a big hint of an Avoidant Coping Mode. Worksheet 10, "My Avoidant Coping Mode" can be of help. You need to find out how you would feel if you did not give in to your annoying habit.

4.2.2   How can I detect Avoidant Coping Mode in others?

An Avoidant Coping Mode is usually easy to detect in other people. When you sense that someone is always ducking out of things, or when they never attend social events although they agreed to come; when someone always keeps raising issues in a meeting

Worksheet 10: My Avoidant Coping Mode

My Avoidant Coping Mode

My ways to avoid	Typical situations	Why do I behave this way?	What are the origins of my behavior?	What would my Healthy Adult do?

Worksheet 10a: Example of an Avoidant Worksheet

My Avoidant Coping Mode

My ways to avoid	Typical situations	Why do I behave this way?	What are the origins of my behavior?	What would my Healthy Adult do?
I complain about all kind of things and tell others that I am always treated badly. This way I prevent confrontation and change	At work, when I believe my performance is not well enough. When I am dissatisfied with my partner	People are understanding and support me. They give me attention and sympathy	My mom always complained about her bad marriage. It was difficult for me, but this way she could go on with her marriage and didn't have to change anything	My Healthy Adult would try to change the situation by talking to my boss and partner about my problems in order to get my needs met in a better way.

although the discussion is finished and all tasks have been assigned; when someone fails to register for exams over and over again… in all these cases avoidance is playing an important role.

When you get to know the person a little better you might get an insight on how their avoidance works. Maybe a friend often fails to show up at a party because he always "forgets about it" while sitting in front of the computer. Or you realize that your friend always starts drinking heavily as soon as she arrives at a party because she feels so anxious.

Take a moment to think about avoidant patterns that you have encountered in people around you in the last few weeks. You may have a glance at Box 4.2 as a prompt. You will be surprised by the omnipresence of avoidance!

Avoidance in interaction. Like many other Modes, Avoidant Modes usually contribute to long-lasting, damaging vicious circles. On the one hand, people may be upset by your chronic avoidant behaviors; on the other, avoidance may prevent you pursuing your goals – in your job or your private life. People with strong Avoidant Modes often do not have satisfying relationships!

The core feelings behind avoidance are usually rejection, threat, or lack of attachment. People may settle into their Avoidant Modes over years, stay socially isolated and experience very few positive emotions in their relationships. Crucially, the dysfunctional coping leads to an increase of those negative emotions which initiated this Mode…

Case Example

Harry (see case example 1, p. **83**) is in his third term at university. At the beginning of his studies he made fewer new acquaintances than most of his fellow students because he avoided social situations such as parties or other student gatherings. Now he feels that everyone else knows each other, but he still doesn't belong. He feels awful about this, and his avoidance becomes even stronger.

He suffers from a similar pattern with his exams, assignments, and tests. Most of the other students keep up quite well with the schedule, but Harry has already piled up a backlog of exams and assignments to be done: he feels helplessly overstrained, ashamed and inferior to the other students. Of course, this further increases his avoidance! He can hardly stop ruminating and is no longer sleeping well – he shows the first clinical signs of depression.

4.3   Overcompensatory Coping Mode

When we talk about overcompensation, we talk about people who behave as if the opposite of the messages of their Parent Modes and Child Modes were true. They may behave very self-confidently although they actually feel insecure; or they may behave in a highly dominant and assertive manner, sometimes aggressive or controlling: they show off, they attack others, although they may actually feel inferior or helpless. Not all overcompensating is associated with inner feelings of insecurity or inferiority, however; some people who are assertive, controlling, or dominant may feel strong, intelligent, and superior.

Sometimes we talk about "contraphobic" behaviors. People with contraphobic behaviors initiate situations or experiences they actually find extremely distressing or hard to deal with.

In Box 4.3 we list some typical overcompensatory patterns.

4.3.1   How can I detect Overcompensatory Coping Mode in myself?

The following statements will help you to estimate whether you tend to show signs of overcompensatory behavior:

- I can be very critical about what others do or don't do.
- I fantasize about becoming famous, rich, important, or successful.

Box 4.3: Typical Overcompensatory Behavior Patterns

- **Narcissistic arrogance**. These people present themselves as brilliant and superior. They look down on others, assuming an air of intelligence and success. Other people find them arrogant and show-offs.
- **Paranoid control**. People with a Paranoid Overcontrolling Coping Mode are very suspicious of others. They believe that they are being taken advantage of, so they seek to protect themselves against attacks. They cope with their feelings of threat by blaming and controlling others. They are always easily persuaded that others conspire against them.
- **Obsessive control**. Sometimes people who actually feel insecure insist on telling others what to do. They take strong control of a situation to arrange things "in the right way." People with this type of overcompensation come across as stubborn and inflexible.
- **Attention-seeking**. Attention-seeking behavior was formerly called "**hysterical**." These people force everyone to treat them as the center of attention. They display superficial signs of high emotion, and cannot bear anyone else being a subject of interest (**histrionic personality disorder**).
- **Aggression**. Aggressive overcompensation is typical of people who have experienced severe violence and threat in their past. People in an aggressive overcompensation Mode will typically try to seize control of a group or situation by physical violence or verbal intimidation. They may use threats or violence deliberately to take revenge on other people or even eliminate them.
- **Cheating and cunning**. People who grew up in a very insecure environment sometimes learned to lie and to manipulate others to enforce their own interests. This type of behavior in an adult is typical of cheating overcompensation.

- If I am criticized I jump to my defense.
- I tend to overrule and control others.
- I get respect by threatening others.

It can be complicated to detect overcompensation in yourself. Unlike most of the other Modes we are dealing with in this book (except Healthy Adult and Happy Child Mode), you may not feel

---

Case Examples

1. **Narcissism.** Glenn works as a senior physician in a psychiatric clinic. His team often feels stressed and even bullied by him because he tends to criticize and humiliate colleagues in front of the whole team. Glenn is too sure of himself. He often makes a great show of interfering in the treatment of a patient he doesn't even know. However, it's not possible to stand up to Glenn as he always reacts with more criticism and humiliation. Behind closed doors his team calls him "The Lord God."

2. **Obsessive control.** Olivia is in the third year of her studies and has to prepare oral presentations with fellow students. Cooperation is always extreme stressful for Olivia, who tries to control everything. She often takes over most of the work, assigns tasks to the others in a very dominant manner, and makes rigid demands on her colleagues. She can hardly bear when the slides do not exactly look "her" way. In meetings she talks most of the time and can hardly be interrupted. It only makes things worse when others advise her to relax. That makes her talk even faster and be even more rigid. Finally she often does everything by herself, and her colleagues are not even grateful for that...

3. **Aggression.** Carolyn experienced severe physical and sexual abuse when she was a child. In adolescence she got involved with drugs, temporarily lived on the street, and worked as a prostitute. She is a physically tough woman who easily becomes loud and aggressive and always gets her way. When someone asks critical questions or makes a critical comment, she immediately flicks into attack. She insults and accuses the other person, and sometimes even threatens them with physical attack.

4. **Paranoid control.** John has been admitted to a clinic for drug abusers. Thus, he has become dependent on the people who are trying to help him. However, he mistrusts everyone, especially therapists and social workers. During his youth attended a boarding school and was frequently sexually abused. Since then he has kept everyone at a distance and never shows his feelings. He is constantly "scanning" his therapist and is upset by every unexpected change. He refuses to participate in parts of the program. He constantly monitors social workers' punctuality and complains bitterly when they are tardy or miss an appointment.

5. **Cheating and cunning.** Kevin grew up in a trailer park. He had a chaotic youth and he was severely emotionally neglected, but materially spoilt. He was a lively and naughty child who needed limits, but his parents did not set them. His mother was an alcoholic and his father left the family when Kevin was two years old. His mother had several partners and neglected Kevin. He was partly raised by his grandparents. When he was 14 years old he got a trailer of his own and had a life on his own. He was always cheating and often used cunning and deceit to make sure his needs were met. He became increasingly involved in illegal activities and started using and dealing drugs.

too bad when in an Overcompensatory Mode. Sometimes you may even feel very good about yourself: smarter than all the others, or in control of the situation. This is the very nature of overcompensation! It seems often to work very well in helping you achieve your goals.

However, when looking more deeply most people feel that overcompensation is not *only* pleasant. The often do not feel really in touch with themselves whilst overcompensating. They do not feel certain of what they actually need or want, and they are certainly not relaxed. On some level they often do not like this state of self. Maybe they sense that they are talking too much or that they show off – but they may not have a clue on how to stop it.

Like all other Coping Modes, Overcompensatory Coping Mode often becomes active in distressing situations. If you suspect that you sometimes react with overcompensation, try to think back to a distressing situation. Remember how you felt and how you reacted. Is it possible that you showed signs of overcompensation? Work sheet 11, "My Overcompensatory Coping Mode" can help you with this question.

When other people criticize you because of typical overcompensatory behaviors, you should take it seriously. Maybe people have already told you that you are egoistic, a show off, dominant, bossy, or way too loud or too excitable. You should check whether that behavior happened in the context of overcompensation. Try to imagine the situation in question. Were there vulnerable feelings hidden behind the dominant or aggressive face? When you have indeed been accused of such things but can't remember a specific incident, just go and ask a good friend. They will certainly be able to give you a good example if there is one.

4.3.2   How can I detect Overcompensatory Coping Mode in others?

Usually it's much easier to detect overcompensation in others than in oneself. People in overcompensatory Mode come across as agitated or fake; they show off, or try to take control

Worksheet 11: My Overcompensatory Coping Mode

My Overcompensatory Coping Mode

Which of the following behaviors seem familiar to me?	How intensive is this pattern? (0–100)	In which situations do I behave this way?	What is my actual need in this situation?	Is this need met by my behavior?
Narcissistic patterns				
Paranoid control				
Obsessive control				
Attention seeking				
Aggression				
Falseness, trickiness				

over others. The recipients of their behavior will usually feel defensive, controlled, or even threatened. In the case of narcissistic overcompensation, the objects of the overcompensatory actions and words may feel devalued, because the other person plays the "big shot." We usually dislike such states in other people, but, because we are afraid of their reaction, we often do not tell them. Indeed, the person is likely to react to criticism with further overcompensation – more bossy, controlling, or aggressive. Most people remain silent because they do not want to become a target of yet more overcompensation.

Again, this is a vicious circle, as with most dysfunctional modes. People usually develop an overcompensational pattern to cope with intense feelings of loneliness, helplessness, inferiority, or threat. They control threats and set limits to others via their overcompensation. Others, however, will find the overcompensator unlikable and will either draw back or engage in conflicts. This consolidates both the original negative feelings and the overcompensation. People with an Overcompensatory Coping Mode are often lonely and unloved.

Case Example

Juliette has been dating Tom for several months. Both of them were neglected by their parents in childhood. Juliette's parents were very demanding, but never really cared about her. Tom, on the other hand, was physically abused by his parents. He can hardly stand other people being cold or even condescending. Juliette and Tom talk a lot about the past and try to support each other.

One day, Juliette returns home feeling very low. Tom, however, does not notice. He announces a football evening with his buddies the same night. Julia feels misunderstood, hurt, and abandoned by him (Vulnerable Child Mode). Instead of talking about her feelings she coldly says: "Get lost, I don't

> want to see you tonight anyway" (Aggressive Coping Mode). Tom feels hurt and doesn't understand why she is treating him so badly even though she knows all about his vulnerable side. If he were to apply the same Aggressive Coping Mode as Juliette the result would be a flaming row. If he were to resort to an avoiding coping strategy he would leave immediately, giving Juliette the feeling that he was abandoning her.

4.4   Summary

People use different coping styles in different situations. You may discover that you use one of the Coping Modes more frequently than the others. People with a strong Guilt-inducing Parent Mode, for example, may for a long time cope by surrendering. However when it becomes too much they may switch into an Avoidant Coping Mode to spare themselves strong negative emotions. Users of the overcompensating Coping Mode may be less aware of their style, because they often feel very good about themselves, smarter than everybody else, in control of the situation. It is only when they look at the reactions of others that they realize that people in their circle of acquaintances or colleagues feel pushed away or controlled. When other people tell someone that they are egoistic, a show-off, dominant, or bossy they're probably describing and criticizing an overcompensatory Mode.

You can reflect on what you have learned about Dysfunctional Coping Modes before completing the third section of Worksheet 1, "My Mode overview."

In the next chapter you will learn how you can cope with difficult situations in a healthy way without being overwhelmed by strong emotions or negative inner voices. This Mode is called the "Healthy Adult Mode."

5

Healthy Adult Mode

The Healthy Adult Mode is your internal superior authority. It has a fairly objective, reasonable overview of your emotions and other psychological processes. In psychodynamic therapies this Mode is called the "healthy ego function." In this Mode you have a healthy, adequate view of yourself and others. You can deal with everyday problems without getting into emotional troubles; small signs of rejection will not upset you too much, because they do not mean the world to you; you can tolerate conflicts and deal with them. However, you also know that you sometimes have to compromise and put your own needs and desires into second place. Overall, you can keep a healthy balance between your own needs and those of other people. Since you are not overwhelmed by negative feelings in this Mode, you don't have to avoid or overcompensate your feelings; you usually have at least some idea how you feel and why your current feelings have been triggered; you feel (mostly) adult – you can pursue adult interests, responsibilities, and pleasures. Of course we are talking about the big picture here – nobody is perfect!

Maybe you have already noticed that the Healthy Adult and the Happy Child have some things in common. The main thing is that you feel generally well and relaxed in either of these two Modes. In the Happy Child the main feelings are ease, fun, and curiosity. In contrast, in the Healthy Adult Mode you experience more adult pleasures, but also responsibilities and challenges.

Breaking Negative Thinking Patterns: A Schema Therapy Self-Help and Support Book,
First Edition. Gitta Jacob, Hannie van Genderen and Laura Seebauer.
© 2011 Beltz Psychologie in der Verlagsgruppe
Beltz • Weinheim Basel. Published 2015 by John Wiley & Sons, Ltd.

Box 5.1: Features of the Healthy Adult Mode

- "Healthy ego functioning"
- Realistic judgment of situations, conflicts, relationships, yourself, and other people
- Little problems do not trigger overwhelming negative emotions
- You sense both your own feelings and needs and those of other people
- You can balance your needs with the needs of others
- You can make commitments, take responsibilities, and comply to your duties
- You find constructive solutions for problems
- You enjoy adult pleasures and interests (sports, culture, sex, etc.)

People with a strong Happy Child Mode usually experience a strong Healthy Adult Mode, and vice versa. In people with strong Dysfunctional Child and Parent Modes, however, the Healthy Adult Mode is often underdeveloped. It's no wonder that people with a strong Healthy Adult Mode suffer less from psychological problems than those with weak Healthy Adult Modes.

An important precondition for the development of a strong Healthy Adult Mode is the fulfillment of basic human and child needs in childhood and adolescence (see Chapter 2, p. **10**). When a child feels loved and attached; when they experience the right to express their needs and feelings freely; when their autonomy is accepted, but they also experience limits – these are the bases of a Healthy Adult Mode. Unfortunately, it works both ways – people who did not have these positive experiences find it much harder to develop a strong Healthy Adult Mode.

Case Examples

1. You already know Anne from Section 2.3 about the Happy Child Mode. She and her husband are both working and jointly care for their three children. They have strong Happy Child Modes – but they also need a strong Healthy Adult Mode to balance their responsibilities and needs.

    It is important for them to set priorities, in order to keep on track despite all daily hassles and problems. Moreover, they are able to take care of their kids, but can also express their needs for relaxation and recovery. Thanks to their Healthy Adult Mode they have enough discipline to exercise regularly – sport is very important for psychological stability. Of course they are not perfect – but altogether things work well for them.

2. **Emma.** You have already heard about Emma, who is fond of kids, in Section 2.3. For years she has been committed to her job with passion and she's tended to sacrifice a little too much. After suffering from a herniated disk she learned to take better care of herself, instead of putting all her energy in taking care of others. Today she integrates phases of recovery in her daily life. She has started walking and has a sauna regularly. Moreover, she has put a little more distance between herself and some friends who were often very demanding, asking her for help but not caring about her needs.

5.1   How can I detect a Healthy Adult Mode in myself?

In Healthy Adult Mode you feel well and relaxed (at least to some degree). You may have worries, but you don't feel overwhelmed by daily hassles; you have good contact with yourself, i.e. you are able to sense your current feelings and needs –you can access your inner experiences. In Healthy Adult Mode you are not tense; you don't need avoidance or exaggerated surrendering to deal with problems or conflicts.

The following sentences characterize the Healthy Adult Mode:

- I know when I should talk about my feelings and when I should not.
- I can solve problems rationally, without being overwhelmed by my feelings.
- I have enough stability and safety in my life
- When I feel unjustly criticized, abused, or exploited, I can protect myself.

Many people aim to promote and enforce their Healthy Adult Mode. Think about the situations where you have easy access to this Mode: these will be good starting points to develop and strengthen it! Worksheet 12, "My Healthy Adult Mode," can help you with this.

- What activities or situations are related to my Healthy Adult Mode?
- Are there some people in my life who help me to access my Healthy Adult Mode?
- How do I feel in my Healthy Adult Mode?

Try to get a feeling for the factors supporting your Healthy Adult Mode. By the way, no one is always in their Healthy Adult Mode – that would be an unrealistic goal!

5.2 How can I detect a Healthy Adult Mode in others?

The Healthy Adult Mode is activated when you deal realistically and adequately with your problems. You have a clear view of things and aren't hindered by exaggerated self-criticism (Punitive Parent Mode), by extreme vulnerability (Vulnerable Child Mode), or by attempts to avoid or overcompensate emotions.

Worksheet 12: My Healthy Adult Mode

My Healthy Adult Mode
My name for this Mode (e.g. Responsible Peter):
1. How can I realize that my Healthy Adult Mode is present?   What is **triggering** my Healthy Adult Mode?
Which **feelings** do I usually have in this Mode?
Which **thoughts** tend to come up in this Mode?
Which **memories** are associated/get triggered?
2. Are my basic **needs** met when I am in the Healthy Adult Mode?
3. How does this Mode affect my feelings of safety?

You can address critical issues or conflicts, and the people you're dealing with won't get it all wrong or overreact. With regard to your relationships the Healthy Adult Mode resembles the Happy Child Mode: while Dysfunctional Parent and Child Modes often trigger negative feelings, burdening and straining a relationship, the Healthy Adult Mode works in exactly the opposite way, enabling good, resilient relationships, and making successful cooperation with others possible. Conflicts do not lead to a total breakdown. People with a strong Healthy Adult Mode not only have relatively few psychological problems, they are also popular and can build and maintain relationships and friendships with others. Their competence in living a self-determined (social) life strengthens their Healthy Adult Mode. Positive feedback is a virtuous circle.

5.3   How can I distinguish the Healthy Adult Mode from other modes?

You have probably noticed that it can be complicated to distinguish precisely all the Modes that you have read about so far. The Healthy Adult Mode serves the fulfillment of responsibilities and duties – but how does is differ from the Guilt-inducing Parent Mode that has a tight focus on fulfilling assignments? The Healthy Adult Mode is able to express annoyance – but what about the Angry Child Mode, expressing a lot of anger? What about the avoidance of feelings? When is it dysfunctional, and when might it actually be functional to avoid certain situations, people, or feelings?

These questions are important. Sometimes the Mode in the foreground is hard to identify – several Modes can be activated simultaneously. For instance, I may feel hurt and rejected (Vulnerable Child Mode) although my head is telling me that the other person likes me and doesn't want to reject me (Healthy Adult Mode).

Nevertheless, there is an important rule of thumb to find out whether it's your Healthy Adult Mode or one of the dysfunctional

Modes that is active. The key, again, is a consideration of your needs. When both your needs and the needs of others are met in a given situation, the Healthy Adult Mode is active. Note that having a good sense of your own and others' feelings and needs is important. However, when you are mainly acting upon your own needs, not greatly or at all caring about the needs of others – or when you do not have a sense of your needs at all – then Dysfunctional Modes are active.

Table 5.1   An overview of Functional and Dysfunctional Modes

	Healthy Adult Mode	*Dysfunctional Mode*
Self-discipline	Fulfills duties and is disciplined, but watches out for limits and needs. *Example*: He is ambitious and fulfills assignments but can also take breaks and leaves time for recovery.	Demanding Parent Mode; overstrains and demands to much discipline. *Example*: He is ambitious and works around the clock, has no interests outside work, runs high risk of burn-out.
Self-criticism	Can criticize themselves, but without self-hatred. *Example*: Can detect own weaknesses and tries to work on it; doesn't think she's worthless.	Punitive Parent Modes; exaggerates self-criticism, hate themselves, block themselves by prohibitions. *Example*: Thinks she is worthless as soon as any weakness becomes visible.
Pleasure, overdoing things	Knows that it is important to enjoy things and not always be disciplined; but doesn't exaggerate. *Example*: Grants himself a luxurious dinner from time to time or buys expensive shoes just for pleasure. However expenses are never beyond reasonable limits.	Undisciplined, Impulsive, Spoilt Child Mode; fulfills own needs without consideration of others or long-term consequences. *Example*: He buys new clothes all the time despite being in debt.

Table 5.1   (*Continued*)

	Healthy Adult Mode	Dysfunctional Mode
Expression of anger	Expresses anger in a socially adequate way. *Example*: Tells her boyfriend in private why she is upset.	Angry Child Mode; has uncontrolled outbursts of anger with negative consequences. *Example*: She explodes out of nothing at a party after anger has been accumulating for some time.
Avoidance of feelings	Can use avoidance as a strategy but is not hindered by extreme avoidance. *Example*: Is in contact with own feelings but "switches off" when the moody boss has a bad day and starts screaming.	Avoidant Coping Mode; avoids any kind of emotion and keeps the person from important relationships, experiences, and developments. *Example*: Is afraid of criticism and therefore keeps distance in all contacts, also towards friends and reliable, friendly people.
Taking control	Does not fear taking control, but stays flexible and takes the interests of others into account. *Example*: Takes over command when it becomes obvious that things are not coordinated, leaves the command happily to others when things work out.	Overcompensatory Mode; fixates and repeats on control, imposes control on others; is very inflexible. *Example*: Always commands everything; everyone around is annoyed.

5.4   Summary

In this chapter you have discovered how the Healthy Adult Mode feels, thinks and acts. This Mode, together with the Happy Child Mode, gives you a good feeling about yourself and others and helps you to attain your goals. You can put information about the Healthy Adult Mode into Worksheet 1, the Mode Overview.

In the second part of this book we will explain how you can change your persistent patterns by weakening Dysfunctional Modes, supporting your Child Modes and making your Healthy Adult and Happy Child stronger. Table 5.1 is an overview of Functional and Dysfunctional Modes.

Part II
Change Your Modes

6

Healing Vulnerable Child Modes

It was good old Sigmund Freud who said that the most important goal of therapy was to learn to be a good mother and a good father to yourself. We think that two issues are particularly important for this: first, you have to get in touch with your Vulnerable Child Mode; second, you must learn to take good care of it.

Getting in touch with your Vulnerable Child Mode may not be that easy for you. Many people have difficulties remembering their childhood, or they find it distressing to deal with childhood memories. Many people even reject their Child Mode, even up to the point of actually hating it, because of the negative feelings that come with it. Unfortunately, this attitude doesn't do anything to decrease your problematic emotions…

The second step – learning to take good care of your Vulnerable Child Mode – may also be quite a challenge. An important precondition for good care is that you accept your "inner child" even though it might be difficult at times. Try to find out what the real needs of your inner child are. As time goes by you will come to better understand what it's telling you.

Breaking Negative Thinking Patterns: A Schema Therapy Self-Help and Support Book, First Edition. Gitta Jacob, Hannie van Genderen and Laura Seebauer.
© 2011 Beltz Psychologie in der Verlagsgruppe
Beltz • Weinheim Basel. Published 2015 by John Wiley & Sons, Ltd.

6.1   Get Acquainted with your Vulnerable Child Mode

There are different ways of getting in touch with your Vulnerable Child Mode. One of the best ways is through so called *imagery exercises*. In these exercises you connect your feelings with images or ideas in your imagination. Our feelings and memories are closely linked to each other. When you suffer from inner child feelings such as sadness or loneliness, an inner journey into the past (an imagery exercise) may help you to understand the origin of these feelings.

Exercise 6.1

Get in Touch with your Vulnerable Child Mode

Close your eyes and relax. Take a deep breath. Feel how your breath flows in and out.

Let your mind wander to a recent situation when you had negative feelings which were possibly linked to your Vulnerable Child Mode. Relive the situation and feel the emotions as intensely as possible. When you can feel the related emotions, erase the current situation from your inner screen and let your mind wander into your past. Wait to see the images or memories that turn up… sense the feelings of the child you were when you experienced these memories.

Are these feelings somehow related to the emotions you're reliving today?

Case Example

Maddison is a middle school teacher with a strong Vulnerable Child Mode. It originates from her experience of being bullied at school. In her job the Child Mode is triggered when she has conflicts with her students.

Today she had to teach three lessons in a very defiant 9th grade. In the afternoon she feels exhausted, rejected, lonely, and desperate. Lying on a couch she closes her eyes, accepts, and senses these emotions. Then she lets her mind wander back to her childhood. After a few seconds a mental image pops up – a memory that she had forgotten all about. While on a class trip she had stumbled and fallen and broken her glasses. Without her glasses her journey back to school and then home had been difficult for her: her teacher had to hold her hand. The other kids made fun of her, and at home her mother did not comfort her, but instead was upset because of the trouble and expense of replacing the broken glasses. Her feelings were very similar to those she felt today.

Maybe you are afraid to get in touch with your inner Child Mode through the path of reliving a distressing situation. Exercise 6.2 illustrates another good way of access. In this exercise you slowly approach and make contact with your "little self."

After exercise 6.2 you may ask yourself some questions:

- What did the encounter with your "little self" feel like? Take some notes of the feelings and thoughts evoked by this exercise.
- What did your "little self" want you to do? What did it need?
- Was there something that you wanted to give your "little self"? Maybe an object such as a blanket, or some advice, or comfort?

You may vary this exercise if you wish. You could visit your "little self" in your former home or meet it at some other significant place. You can take a walk around the house where you grew up, and maybe meet other people who were important to you (parents, brothers and sisters, classmates, teachers etc.).

Get in touch with memorabilia. Objects like old toys, letters, or pictures are also helpful in your attempt to get in touch with the feelings you had as a child. Our memories and feelings are

Exercise 6.2

An Imagery Journey to your "Little Self"

For this exercise it's important that you are sitting in a quiet place where you are comfortable and relaxed. Make sure that you won't be disturbed for the next 15 minutes. Read the complete set of instructions to this exercise first. Then close your eyes and relax

Imagine you're walking on a country lane. Green lawns are to your left and right, the sun is shining, and a gentle breeze is blowing. You walk along the lane as it winds around a hill so that you can see just 100 yards or so ahead. Imagine how you're walking; feel the sun and the breeze on your face. Stick with that image until you are calm and completely relaxed.

After you've been walking for some time you see a little child walking towards you from behind the hill. The child is maybe five or six years old. You keep walking slowly and the child comes closer. You realize that this child is you. Your "little self" comes closer and closer. Take your time to look at it as you come to each other. When you finally meet, take the time to say a friendly hello. Maybe you want to hug it or pat its hair. Or it might be that you want to keep some distance at first. Try to imagine the scene in as much lifelike detail as you can. What does your "little self" look like? How do you feel about meeting it? Is there something you want to tell your "little self"? Or perhaps you just sit next to each other on the grass for a time. Spend a few minutes on this encounter, then, when you feel that it's the right moment, say good-bye to your "little self." Do you want to pass something along? You watch your "little self" departing slowly. Finish the exercise at your own speed... sense what your body feels like in your chair and feel your feet touching the floor. Then open your eyes slowly and return into the here and now.

closely linked to sensations. The smell of a certain perfume can bring a memory of your grandmother to life; an old picture can evoke a scene from your childhood. Try to sense the feelings associated to these objects as vividly as possible. If you understand the origin of your feelings, you also may find an understanding why certain situations evoke distressing feelings today.

Case Example

After the horrible meeting when he stumbled over the flip chart Daniel (see Section 2.1.) examined his feelings on his way home. He'd already had a vague idea that there might be a connection between his experiences at school and the intense shame and helplessness he sometimes experienced as an adult. At home he searched out a box with school stuff from his basement and found an old picture of the whole class with the teacher who had teased him so badly. Little Daniel in the picture seems to be feeling pretty miserable. Daniel becomes very sad and angry because "Little Daniel" had such a hard time at school. In his imagery he returns into these memories. Then he imagines that he enters the school scene as the adult man he has become. He finds Little Daniel and comforts and hugs him. This experience makes him sad, but also gives him a sense of relief and a feeling of attachment and safety.

6.2 Taking care of your Vulnerable Child Mode

Accepting and tolerating your feelings. You can only take better care of your vulnerable child part if you accept and tolerate its feelings. Try to find out the needs of your Vulnerable Child Mode.

Exercise 6.3

What Can You do When Your Vulnerable Child Mode Shows Up?

When your Vulnerable Child Mode is triggered, just close your eyes and try to sense what you really want and need now. What needs of yours are not being met right now? Does this remind you of a childhood memory? Can you take better care of those needs today than you could when you were a child?

Figure 6.1   Healthy Adult – Happy Child

Healing Vulnerable Child Modes. The case example of Daniel may give you a first idea of a way that you can heal or comfort your Vulnerable Child Mode with mental images or symbols. Whenever Daniel feels his Vulnerable Child Mode arising, he tries to bring up the mental image of Little Daniel being comforted by Adult Daniel. Not only such images, but also symbols, gestures, and slogans can comfort your Vulnerable Child Mode. It can be very helpful to imagine your "adult self" standing by your "little self" providing comfort.

In imagery exercises you can find healing images of your "adult self" or another good and caring figure taking care of your "little self." The only rule for these images is that the needs of your "little self" have to be fulfilled.

Symbols, images, songs, etc. can help to establish better care for your Vulnerable Child Mode and be a reminder of it in your everyday life. Moreover, it is obviously important to fulfill your current needs for contact, comfort, and fun in the here and now! Finally, your Vulnerable Child Mode can only be really healed when you achieve a feeling of being loved and your needs being met today.

Case Example: Creating an Image of Affiliation

Keira's fellow students are having a party on Saturday night. They invited everybody (including Keira) via e-mail but did not ask Keira personally to come along. Saturday night she can be found sitting alone at home, unhappy and dissatisfied with herself.

To get in touch with her feelings and needs she initiates an imagery exercise, starting from her current feelings. In her memory she slips into a scene when she was about 8 years old. She had just moved to a new town and didn't yet know the other children in her class. After school the other girls played skip rope in the schoolyard. At that time Keira

---

didn't dare to approach them; she walked home feeling lonely and crying. Now she imagines "Adult Keira" coming to the schoolyard and taking her by the hand. "Adult Keira" encourages and reassures "Little Keira." Together they approach the other girls. With the support of "Adult Keira" "Little Keira" is able to ask the girls whether she can play with them. The girls agree and they all play together. "Adult Keira" sits at the side and watches the girls play. Her presence reassures "Little Keira" and makes her feel safe. When Keira finishes the exercise with a feeling of safety and affiliation, she decides to draw a picture of the scene. In the next weeks she just thinks about that picture whenever she starts feeling insecure or lonely. Usually that makes her smile and gives her the courage to get in touch with others. What's more, she decides to join the next party no matter whether she gets a personal invitation or not. Everybody just gets an email, so why not accept it? And as soon as she walks into the next party she can sense a feeling of connection!

If you've already got to know your little Child Mode better, it can be a useful exercise to write them a letter. It may not be easy to start writing this letter. Try to remember what you were missing at that age, and put down what you want to tell your "little self." Think about what you could do today to care for your "inner child."

Case Example: Madison's Letter to "little Maddie"

Dear little Maddie,

You really had a tough life at school. I wish I could travel back in time to protect and support you. On the other hand, I can understand very well why you did not stand up for yourself. Sometimes I still don't even manage to say something when things go wrong for me. Why is it so damned hard for us to stand up for ourselves? I want to tell you that you are important to me and that I will learn to take care of you . . .

Taking better care of yourself. Better care for your vulnerable child is closely linked to self-compassion. If you are self-compassionate, you look at yourself with friendly attention and try to meet your needs. In Chapters 8 and 11 you will find exercises that will help you to get much better at this.

Here are some suggestions for questions you should ask yourself that may help you to adopt a self-compassionate perspective.

- Why do I feel hurt or sad right now?
- What do I need right now?
- (When a Child Mode turns up more often than usual) What is currently wrong in my life?

  Do you have relationship problems, or other distressing issues such as too much work, a move, the experience of a loss? What could comfort you, and help you to find a better balance with your needs?

- The Child Mode comes along with specific emotions, e.g. sadness or loneliness. What do you need to experience the opposite emotion, e.g. joy instead of sadness, or companionship instead of loneliness?

Case Example: Maddison – Learning to Meet her Needs

After the hard day in front of the tough class, Maddison understood that rejection by her students reminded her of being bullied at school. She felt isolated and lonely. She asked herself what she could do to feel less so. This made her think about a colleague she can talk to about the trouble you can experience as a teacher with a difficult class.

Maddie knows that, like her, the colleague had some problematic childhood experiences. So, she calls her the same night just to chat a little bit and arrange an appointment for a coffee next day. It's actually not that important for Maddison to talk about the bad morning she had. All that matters is experiencing the safe and friendly contact with her colleague, which is "balm for her soul."

Be aware of Dysfunctional Parent Modes! You may sometimes find that Vulnerable Child Modes and Punitive or Guilt-inducing Parent Modes are closely connected. When you feel weak, ashamed, or lonely, you may also blame yourself for being such an emotional loser (=Punitive Parent Mode). Stay on the watch for these Dysfunctional Parent Modes and set them limits! In Chapter 9 you will find some strategies that help you deal with a Guilt-inducing or Punitive Parent Mode.

Case Example

After stumbling across the flip chart Daniel retreats to the rest room. His feelings of shame and inferiority begin to decrease, but then he notices some old, familiar thoughts coming up in his mind: "That's a classic Daniel – to expose yourself to such ridicule... If you could just once pay attention. ... And leaving the room afterwards was so unprofessional; it made everything worse! Why the hell can't you stay cool? You're such a loser!"

It's absolutely necessary to fight this inner voice! It certainly doesn't help you to feel better! Your inner child needs support and comfort to grow up and get happier.

You'll find strategies on how to weaken the punitive voice in Chapter 9. Fighting the Punitive Parent will help you to turn towards your inner child. If you can take care of your inner child, in particular with imagery exercises, you'll start feeling better.

7

Gaining Control over Angry and Impulsive Child Modes

Do you want to learn how to deal with your Angry, Enraged, Defiant, Impulsive, or Spoilt Child Mode? Two points are particularly important here: first, you have to identify the needs associated with this Mode; second, you need to find ways to express and fulfill these needs in a healthier way.

Again, these Modes usually originate from childhood. Different patterns can result in the development of these kinds of Modes. Maybe you were treated unfairly by relatives, teachers, or classmates. If so, your Angry Child Mode may pop up today when, once again, you feel mistreated or abused. In these cases anger goes usually along with sadness, loneliness, and other emotions of the Vulnerable Child Mode. Most often, the needs behind these feelings ought to be accepted and taken seriously. However you have to learn to express yourself in a healthier way. It's important to realize your needs early – before they are expressed explosively by your angry Modes.

Bear in mind, though, that Impulsive or Spoilt Child Modes can develop when someone was spoilt as a child and didn't learn to accept discipline. It might be that parents or carers tolerated their child acting in a defiant and recalcitrant way. In some way this can actually be considered as neglect – as children need limits, and setting these limits is part of a parent's duties. So, in these cases it is important to learn to accept limits and become more disciplined. Not all needs can be fulfilled – not for children and not for adults.

Breaking Negative Thinking Patterns: A Schema Therapy Self-Help and Support Book,
First Edition. Gitta Jacob, Hannie van Genderen and Laura Seebauer.
© 2011 Beltz Psychologie in der Verlagsgruppe
Beltz • Weinheim Basel. Published 2015 by John Wiley & Sons, Ltd.

Case Examples

1. **Impulsive Child Mode.** You already know Susie from Section 2.2 – the 21-year-old student with a strong Impulsive Child Mode. She is reckless: she drinks a lot and likes to party excessively. Sometimes she even puts herself in danger (unprotected sex), and she's failing in her studies due to lack of discipline.

   Susie's maternal grandmother is the root of the problem: she spoiled Susie, just as she'd spoiled Susie's mother when she was a child. Susie's mother did not take responsibility for her girl but left nearly everything up to the grandmother. As a result, Susie has never learned to control herself and accept limits; she nearly always follows momentary desires.

   After Susie comes round to seeing that she's lost track of her studies and that her party life doesn't make her all that happy, she starts to see a psychotherapist. The therapist teaches her that although meeting your needs and having fun is important, it's also necessary to perform tasks and take on responsibilities. Finally, you have to find a balance between discipline and fun. Susie has to learn to be more disciplined and accept some limits. This means she has to push back against her desires in the short term so that she can reach important long-term goals. Of course, this will take some time and sometimes it will be frustrating… However, as Susie realizes, it will be very beneficial for her.

2. **Angry Child Mode.** You already know Matthew, the 41-year-old software engineer who was introduced in Section 2.2. He becomes angry all too easily when he feels he's being criticized or treated unfairly: he tries so hard to do his best. Behind his anger is the need to be recognized and accepted. He works at high intensity for long hours, striving for perfection, to try to get this need met.

Matthew has to learn that he doesn't need to be such a perfectionist, and that minor criticism need not be emotionally devastating. When he really gets that message, he will no longer react to criticism so angrily. He also has to learn to set limits for other people – only when he's managed all this will he come to understand that other people like him even if he doesn't function at 100 per cent every minute of every day.

7.1 Get Acquainted with your Angry or Impulsive Child Mode

The first things to do are to recognize and analyze the moment when the Angry or Impulsive Child Mode shows up. Does it come along with feelings of vulnerability? Then it is probably "secondary" to a Vulnerable Child Mode. If vulnerable feelings do not play a role, it's likely "primary" anger and frustration. Worksheet 3, "My Angry/Impulsive Child Mode" (in Section 2.2) can be a support. A good way to get in touch with this Mode is through imagery of a situation when your Angry or Impulsive Child Mode showed up.

Exercise 7.1

Close your eyes, focus on your breath, and relax.

Go back into a situation when your Angry or Impulsive Child Mode was in action. Imagine that you are back in this situation. Explore your feelings. Can you feel anger or rage? Or is it mainly indiscipline and frustration? How intense are your feelings? Do you also sense other emotions such as sadness, loneliness, or rejection? Do you feel unfairly or badly treated? If yes, by whom? Would it also be unfair if this person treated other people the same way?

If sadness and vulnerability play a role or if you feel mistreated, this is a hint that a Vulnerable Child Mode is involved. Exercise 6.2 can also help you to find that out.

If you become aware of a Vulnerable Child Mode playing an important role, you should take good care of it. People with both vulnerable and Angry Child Modes often find that rage and anger suddenly disappear when the needs of the Vulnerable Child are met. Sometimes you don't even have to deal with rage and anger as a separate issue. Just go back to the exercises for healing the Vulnerable Child Mode (Exercise 6.2). An Angry Child Mode can even be helpful here, as it teaches you not to neglect your needs. Moreover, you can learn which situations are particularly difficult for the Vulnerable Child Mode.

When an Angry Child Mode is in the foreground, or if your rage and anger are at a dangerous level, exercises 7.2 may be helpful. But always keep in mind that the needs of the Angry or Impulsive Child Mode are often justified, at least to some extent. It's all about the degree and the way that these needs are expressed.

7.2   Setting Limits to Angry or Impulsive Child Modes

After reading the last few pages, would you say that you sometimes show spoilt, impulsive, defiant, or angry patterns? If your answer is yes, it might be important to cut them back – depending on their severity of course! And don't forget that a desire for pleasure or the spontaneous expression of frustration are basically normal – you only have to work on them if you sometimes express them in an exaggerated way.

If you wonder whether your reactions are exaggerated, have a look at their effects on the people around you. For example, is your partner telling you that they feel frustrated by your attitude, and calling you defiant? Do friends or family complain repeatedly about you being egoistic? If that's the case, you should think about working on those patterns. Try to be honest with yourself and take into account that people rarely make a big issue of egoism or defiance. Most people most of the time draw back from someone they find egoistic or spoilt; they wouldn't take the trouble to confront them. As a rule you bring yourself to address

Biographical Origins

As you already know from earlier chapters, it's always worth-while finding out how your Spoilt, Angry, or Impulsive Child Mode developed. The following aspects are very common:

- **Combination with a Vulnerable Child Mode.** Angry or Impulsive Child Modes can show up as a "secondary" Mode when you feel intensely hurt or rejected.
- **Insufficient autonomy**. Many people with strong defiant or Angry Child Modes report that their most important attachment figures, usually parents, did not grant them enough autonomy. Examples would be a mother insisting on choosing the clothes for her teenage son, parents interfering in their children's friendships, or parents making shaming or belittling comments in the presence of friends or relatives. If you experienced a denial of autonomy or unfair treatment as you grew up you'll know that it often provoked defiant behavior patterns, and that sometimes you became "stuck" in those patterns. Such reactions can show up again later in life, even if by then no one actually has the power to take away your autonomy or freely abuse or belittle you.
- **Role models for angry or impulsive behavior**. Learning problematic behavior from observation of other people is a form of social learning through role models (**vicarious learning**). For example, if your father used to react impulsively or aggressively or expressed his needs no matter what the circumstances, you will inevitably have learned that this is normal behavior. No wonder that in adult life you act in a similar way– you just never learnt any better.
- **Lack of limits in childhood**. Sometimes parents fail to set sufficient limits for their children. They may do so because they want to give their children everything they can, or they may be trying to avoid conflicts with the children. They prefer the "easy way." Unfortunately they don't see that children need limits and mustn't be spoilt. It is important for children to learn to be disciplined and to cut back on their own needs, at least sometimes and to a sensible degree. It is important for healthy adult people to accept their limits. Maybe you were unfortunate enough to have been spoilt as a child. Now you have to catch up on the job of setting limits.

this kind of problem only with people who are really important to you. Our assumption is as follows: if more than two people have given you similar negative feedback they might have a point. Of course not *every* negative feedback should be something to dwell on – it may just be the result of a specific situation and have no connection with your personality. Nevertheless, when it comes your way this kind of social information needs to be taken seriously.

7.2.1   Goals and needs

Take a moment to reflect on what you want to accomplish in your life and how your Angry or Impulsive Child Mode is interfering with your progress. Make a list of the advantages and disadvantages of your Angry or Impulsive Child Mode. Worksheet 4, "Advantages and disadvantages of my Angry/Impulsive Child Mode," will help you with this and enable you to get a clear picture. You should note that the list of advantages reveals the obstacles you are going to deal with when you set out to change this Mode.

Case Example: Advantages and Disadvantages of an Obstinate Child Mode

We encountered Ethan in Section 2.2 – boyfriend of Lucy, spoilt as a child and now selfish, unhelpful and easily distracted. Here is his listing of the pros and cons of his behavior pattern:

Advantages of my defiant, Obstinate Child Mode:

- I don't have to deal with annoying stuff.
- I feel that I'm right when I am pig-headed with my girlfriend Lucy. Her anger and frustration hardly reach me. Acting like this is somehow comfortable for me.
- Overall, I manage to hold annoying tasks at arm's length.

Disadvantages of this Mode:

- I don't complete important things. That makes daily life complicated at times and I am frustrated with myself.
- This pattern is bad for my relationships. Lucy, who is very loving and understanding, doesn't deserve to be treated like this.
- I am behaving childishly and I don't like that. I am an adult and I want to behave accordingly.
- I've noticed already, several times, that this Mode interferes with my work. I will not progress if I continue like this. My colleagues and supervisors cannot take me seriously and are more and more annoyed with me.

7.2.2   Chair dialogues

In therapy, this kind of pro–con-argument is often dealt with in a so called "chair dialogue." We use two chairs for the two perspectives – the pros of the Angry Child Mode, and the cons, representing the Healthy Adult point of view. The patient expresses one perspective from the first chair then moves across and responds from the other. If you go through this procedure you'll find that you can develop a clearer understanding of your inner conflicts and make a good start in figuring out your real goals. This method isn't going to work when you are beside yourself with anger, though; you must wait till your fury has cooled down before you can explain the point of view of your Angry Child.

Some people carry out such chair dialogues by themselves, outside the context of therapy. Just try it out, even if it feels silly in the beginning! Sometimes you may find it easier to use two symbols, puppets, or soft toys, instead of chairs. One soft toy (e.g. a cheeky monkey or a crocodile) represents the Undisciplined Child Mode and the other (maybe a teddy bear?) symbolizes the Healthy Adult Mode. Now you can perform a little puppet theater and let the two exchange arguments.

Figure 7.1   Angry Child Mode

7.2.3   *Learn to direct your behavior*

Angry, Enraged Child Mode. If you want to change your Angry or Enraged Child Mode, the biggest challenge is to control anger and rage in provoking situations. If you think that this might be difficult, you're absolutely right! But that doesn't mean that it's impossible… you can change your Angry Child reactions into more appropriate and healthy behaviors – step by step. The basis for this change is to be in touch with your Angry Child Mode (see Worksheet 3, "My Angry/Impulsive Child Mode"). The aim

Case Example

You already know Florence from Section 2.2. Her Angry Child Mode pops up when she feels exploited or ignored. She makes a list of situations that typically trigger her Angry Child Mode and adds notes about her related needs:

When does my Angry Child get triggered?	What need of mine is frustrated in the situation?
I come home and see that the children have just thrown their jackets in the hall instead of hanging them on the cloth hook. My reaction: I slam the door behind me and hang the jackets myself, feeling a lot of anger.	I feel exploited by my children. I would like them to support and unburden me by carrying out small duties.
My children complain that I am too tired to go to the swimming pool with them. My reaction: I scream at them that I had to work all night. Then I start crying.	I feel that my commitment (working night shift to care for the kids at daytime) is not rewarded or appreciated. I feel. On the other hand, it is not my kids' role to appreciate my effort – that's rather up to my husband!
My husband watches football with his friends although I had a bad day and really need his support. My reaction: I yell at him and tell him to get lost.	I need some support and attention. I would really like to talk about my day and feel that my husband understands me.

Florence realizes that the situations triggering her Angry Child Mode have something in common: they are almost always associated with her family. This is a useful basis on which to plan a little experiment, something we like to call a "behavior experiment."

is to know when your Angry Child Mode is triggered, and what needs are at the center of these situations (e.g. autonomy or recognition).

Behavior experiments. Behavior experiments are an excellent way to try out new ways of dealing with difficult situations. It is important that you regard such an experiment as a challenging game to break through fixed behavior patterns. A behavior experiment addresses one of the problematic situations you want to change – in Florence's case situations including outburst of anger or slamming doors.

You start by planning in advance to behave differently the next time such a situation comes up. The new "experimental" behavior can be a constructive attempt to solve the situation in a healthier way – or it can be a funny or exaggerated reaction.

Case Example

For Florence it's easy to choose a situation for her behavior experiment. She is frequently confronted with situations in which she feels exploited and ignored by her children. When she reaches her front door the next day she already is aware of the chaos awaiting her inside. She takes a deep breath and enters the hallway. As expected, all the children's jackets are lying on the floor. She takes another deep breath, takes off her jacket and throws it on top of the pile. Her youngest daughter comes running in the hall to welcome her mother and watches the scene – stunned and irritated. Finally, mother and daughter burst out laughing.

7.2.4   How can I learn to control my anger?

You will certainly need some practice in handling these situations in a healthier way. The following suggestions can help you with this. The goal is to regain control over your reactions and behaviors.

- **Observe early signals**. You know yourself best. What are the early warning signals of your Angry Child Mode? These may be very specific and individual, including bodily sensation (e.g. tensed shoulders) or, thoughts ("I'm fed up with all of this," "You don't give a damn about me"). If you manage to react quickly to those signals you may be able to keep a clear mind instead of exploding with anger. Then you can address the origin of your frustration in a healthier way, which is probably better both for you and for the people around you. Don't delay the expression of anger too much!
- **Express anger stepwise**. Start by expressing your anger calmly. When the other person is still not listening, you may show a little more anger. You are learning to show anger step by step.
- **Take a little break**. Sometimes a short break is the best you can do when you feel the Angry Child coming up. You might stand up in a meeting to open the window and take a deep breath. Or take a very detailed look at the eyebrows and ears of the person in front of you. This kind of short break can help you to become aware what you really want to achieve in the situation (your needs).
- **Use a calming symbol.** Many people find it helpful to prompt themselves with a symbolic object (e.g. a smooth stone to carry in your pocket), a picture (e.g. a lake mirroring the sky), or a certain song that calms them down. Whenever you get into a "critical" situation you can grab your symbolic object in your pocket, imagine looking at the picture, or play your song in your mind… this will help you to relax.
- **Practice alternative behavior in imagery.** You may well have already heard about "mental training." Imagery exercises work pretty much the same way. Imagine a situation that triggers your Angry Child Mode and then imagine in detail how you would react differently. For Florence in the example above this would have been a good alternative option.

"Obstinate" Spoilt Child Mode. It is very important for you to fully understand the advantages and disadvantages of this type of Mode as a preliminary to determining clear goals. A detailed plan will help you. Be aware that this Mode may influence many areas

Exercise 7.3

Imagery Exercise to Limit Anger

Imagine a situation in which you are likely to react with anger. Try to feel the usual emotions.

Make yourself comfortable and make sure that you will not be disturbed.

Think about what would make you feel less angry, and subsequently see how this changes the situation in your mind. It might be, for instance, that you are in need of reassurance from someone; someone telling you that not everybody is restraining or rejecting you. Maybe you can imagine a good friend standing at your side, putting an arm round your shoulder?

Imagine how the situation continues without you expressing intense anger. Instead, imagine yourself staying calm and talking in a clear and measured tone – although it's most important that you still address your needs and point out the limits that have been violated in the situation!

of your life, so you need to choose the domains of your life in which you want to restrict its activity at first. It's going to take you some time to change this Mode substantially.

List critical situations in which you want to set limits to the Obstinate or Spoilt Child Mode. Maybe you want to behave less obstinately with your partner; maybe you've been planning for years to start exercising but you've never managed because your Undisciplined Child Mode does not comply. What do you want to change first?

Try to be realistic and honest with yourself. How difficult will it be to put your specific plan into reality? Some steps might be quite easy – e.g. not to let your partner clean up the breakfast table by herself every day. But others will be much more difficult – e.g. starting a reasonable diet or exercise regime when so far you've only made it as far as walking to the car and you've hated vegetables all your life.

Make a realistic plan of how to implement the changes in your life. Rewarding yourself for successful steps is very important! When you actually manage to change a dysfunctional pattern you deserve to be rewarded. It's a great accomplishment! So, also make a plan on how to reward yourself for passing each of your milestones.

Case Example

Ethan has had some serious arguments with his girlfriend lately. That's why he's decided to become more disciplined and less obstinate. However, this aim in itself won't change anything. He's had to plan concrete goals.

Ethan decides to get two things done weekly – two things that he would normally have delayed doing until his girl-friend took them on. He manages to keep to his plan quite well and his girlfriend is happy with the change. Nonetheless, it's also obvious to both of them that this is just the beginning and that Ethan has to carry on trying to grow.

Don't be too hard with yourself! It's a big step to admit that you act obstinately or like a spoilt child from time to time. This insight deserves respect. You will certainly not change overnight. Of course, you can also keep some of your spoilt habits… but, please, not the ones that hurt or annoy your partner the most. And keep in mind that Modes usually work together; sometimes you have to give priority to dealing with another Mode e.g. your Vulnerable Child Mode or a Dysfunctional Coping Mode. The more you observe and understand all your Modes, the better you will become at setting the right priorities.

8

Strengthen the Happy Child Mode

When your Happy Child Mode has been suppressed or never played an important role in your life, it's particularly important to take things slowly when you do try to get in touch with it. A simple prescription of fun activities ("Just play a little card game and you'll feel great") will probably not work for most people.

It's not often that simple – many people don't even know how to have fun, and with whom. Moreover, they may be afraid that it won't be fun for them anyway as their Punitive Parent Mode would not allow it. But even those people can do a lot to strengthen their Happy Child Mode – they are probably much in need of it! It will not be easy, though, and can't be done all at once.

8.1 Get Acquainted with your Happy Child Mode

Imagery exercises are an excellent way of getting access to your "inner child," no matter which Child Mode we are dealing with. These exercises help you to get in touch with your Happy Child Mode.

Did you notice that it's easier to find activities for your Happy Child Mode today after you've recalled happy memories in an imagery exercise? By contrast, you might feel completely misunderstood (and not have any good answer) if someone asked you

Breaking Negative Thinking Patterns: A Schema Therapy Self-Help and Support Book,
First Edition. Gitta Jacob, Hannie van Genderen and Laura Seebauer.
© 2011 Beltz Psychologie in der Verlagsgruppe
Beltz • Weinheim Basel. Published 2015 by John Wiley & Sons, Ltd.

Exercise 8.1

Get in Contact with your Happy Child Inside

Make yourself comfortable and close your eyes. Relax and focus on your breath.

Think about times when you were happy. Maybe these are childhood memories – a snowy Christmas, a vacation with your favorite aunt, or another particularly happy time. Maybe you'd rather think about more recent situations, such as a trip with friends or family, a special celebration, swimming in a lake... Evoking mental images also evokes the emotions associated with the biographical information of the image.

It's very important that you try to relive the situation with all your senses. If you're thinking about Christmas, you may remember the smell of candles, or the taste of hot chocolate and cookies. If you're remembering swimming in a lake, sense the sun on your skin and the sound of wind in the trees. Such perceptual memories help you to access your positive feelings. Those feelings make it easier to find comparable activities or ideas for your life in the "here and now."

In the next step, let your mind wander... can you think of any activities your Happy Child Mode would like to do today?

in your darkest hour "What makes you really happy? What would you like to do for fun?" It's when you're asked these kind of questions after recalling a happy memory that you will much more likely be able to find an answer.

In psychology, this phenomenon is called an "**affective bridge**." When you recall a happy memory try to build an emotional "bridge" to situations that you can experience today that evoke similar feelings. You may well have observed the affective bridge in others, but it works for everyone, including you.

Case Examples

1. Lisa often feels lonely and sad. Her parents raised her to keep to very rigid norms as part of a strict Christian education. As a result, she is morally hard and disciplined and allows herself almost no pleasures. Her therapist has managed to convince her that the Happy Child Mode should play a bigger role in her life, which is why she's started recalling happy childhood memories. She thinks about trips she took with her community. She feels particularly easy and happy when recalling a trip to the Lakes. The whole group joined together in a boat tour and had ice cream afterwards. Lisa remembers in detail that she had two bowls of ice cream – stracciatella and lemon. Most people would think that those flavors don't fit but Lisa just loved it.

    The next warm day Lisa passes by an ice cream parlor and, on impulse, orders two bowls – stracciatella and lemon. She takes a seat in the sun and enjoys the ice cream. This makes her feel a little melancholy but also peaceful, content and satisfied.

2. Jessica has started dealing with her Happy Child Mode lately. She often wondered which situations might help her to trigger this Mode, and she's noticed that she feels very comfortable around jovial, cheerful women. In an imagery exercise she comes across her jolly aunt Ruby, who gave her the very same feeling. The connection between the past and today makes her smile.

    She decides to make contact with some of the other mothers in her kids' kindergarten: she gets involved in joint activities like organizing the flea market and the cake buffet for the summer party. She doesn't necessarily love those activities, but the contact with the other moms makes her feel comfortable and happy.

8.2   Exercises to Strengthen the Happy Child Mode

The next step is to start and then intensify activities that bring up your Happy Child Mode. As with all things in life it's important to keep the right balance. Obviously, it doesn't make sense to aim to be in your Happy Child Mode all the time: it's essential to take on adult responsibilities and duties. We are most satisfied with our lives when we find a good balance between different activities and needs.

Of course, the situations related to the Happy Child Mode differ from person to person. While some people might love to tinker with their model railroad for hours, others would just hate that. You should start looking for your very own happy child situations. However, some people have no idea how to trigger their Happy Child Mode, especially when it hasn't played a big role in their lives so far. So, look at and think about the list of proposals in the box below. An important feature of Happy Child activities is promoting playfulness and curiosity. Just try something new for a change!

Eliciting the Happy Child

You can trigger your happy child by...

- Falling into a pile of foliage
- Singing loudly, no matter how it sounds
- Racing with children
- Letting the sun shine on your belly
- Doing many somersaults
- Taking a walk in the rain
- Turning up the music
- Starting a pillow fight
- Smiling at other people
- Playing with young animals
- Listening to the sounds of nature
- Eating chocolate cream with a spoon
- Playing tennis on the grass
- Building a cave of blankets
- Having a bath with more bubbles than necessary
- ...

Once you've established the first contact with your Happy Child Mode it will become easier to engage in activities promoting it. You'll know better by now what makes you happy and joyful. This is the time to think about how you want to integrate these feelings in your everyday life. The following points are important:

Promoting the Happy Child Mode needs time! If you just plan on having 10-minute phone calls with aunt Rosie from time to time you will most likely not succeed. First, you won't always reach her when you try, and second, 10 minutes is just not enough – better plan for an hour.

Follow the "principle of small steps"! If you haven't experienced much of the Happy Child Mode in your life so far, it will not burst into flower overnight. You have to care for and be careful with your Happy Child Mode. Be sure of one thing: it will reward you for every small step, and many small steps will take you a long way!

Figure 8.1   Happy Child Mode

Be realistic! People with multiple tasks and stresses often don't have enough spare time to cultivate frequent and long Happy Child spots. In this case it's about making compromises: it's better to go to the swimming pool every second week than never to go at all.

Include other people! If you've got a job and a family to take care of it would be unbalanced to spend many hours by yourself nurturing your Happy Child inside. By the third Saturday in a row you'll be having furious arguments with your kids about it… A good solution is to start Happy Child activities together with your family. They will all love to share your easy fun activities, and the Child Mode is usually at its happiest when it's sharing fun and laughter with others.

Pay attention to your mood! You cannot bring up your Happy Child Mode forcibly. Even though you may have scheduled a slot for the Happy Child Mode it's bound to happen sometime that circumstances interfere with your plans. When you are totally exasperated with things at work it might be better to start with activities to get in touch with the Healthy Adult Mode (for example solving a conflict; see Chapter 5). Make amends with your Happy Child Mode by looking after it when your mood has improved.

We hope that this chapter has helped you to develop some good ideas for your Happy Child Mode. You must spend plenty of time with it and try hard to look after it, particularly when you feel that you have to fight a Dysfunctional Mode (e.g. Punitive Parent Mode).

9

Setting Limits to Dysfunctional Parent Modes

In Chapter 3 you read a lot about Dysfunctional Parent Modes and how they can put you under pressure by making you devalue yourself, feel ashamed of yourself, or become filled with self-hatred. In this chapter we will deal with the question of how to change this, in two steps.

Step one will begin by listing the messages from the Dysfunctional Parent Mode. You'll learn how to find out which critical inner voices are giving you a hard time, where they come from, and what activates them.

In the second step you'll learn how you to set limits to these voices. To achieve this it is important to make a clear distinction between the Healthy Adult and the Dysfunctional Parent Modes. The Healthy Adult is also about challenging yourself, but in the way a good parent would do. The Parent Mode becomes dysfunctional when it is harmful, i.e. it forbids you to take care of your needs or it makes you go past your limits over and over again. Healthy and constructive self-criticism is a positive thing, but destructive self-criticism or self hatred has to be reduced.

Breaking Negative Thinking Patterns: A Schema Therapy Self-Help and Support Book, First Edition. Gitta Jacob, Hannie van Genderen and Laura Seebauer.
© 2011 Beltz Psychologie in der Verlagsgruppe
Beltz • Weinheim Basel. Published 2015 by John Wiley & Sons, Ltd.

9.1   Get in Touch with your Dysfunctional Parent Mode

We have introduced you to the use of imagery exercises to get in touch with your inner child elements. However, you have to be very careful if you're thinking about using imagery exercises to get in touch with your Dysfunctional Parent Modes. Going back into situations related to belittlement, punishment, or abuse can lead to serious negative mood shifts . In severe cases you may need help from a therapist to get out of your lowered mental state. So please take care with the exercises in this chapter, and instead of deep imagery just use rational thinking.

Exercise 9.1

Get in Touch with your Dysfunctional Parent Mode

Make yourself comfortable and try to relax. Think about a situation in the past in which you felt under strong pressure although objectively the situation did not demand it. When did you recently feel strongly rejected, unlikable, forced to do something you actually did not want to do? When was your Parent Mode particularly active?

Now, reflect what the situation was all about. What did you feel you had to do, why did you feel rejected? How would you have felt if you had been able to act in the way you wanted? Would you have felt like a loser, like a traitor? Would you have felt guilty, or sensed that you are not entitled to fight for your rights? The answers to these questions will help you to better understand your Dysfunctional Parent Mode.

If the situation was about feeling like a failure, there was probably a strong Demanding Parent Mode in the background. If the main feeling was guilt, it was very likely a Guilt-inducing Parent Mode. If shame, self-hatred, or intense fear were the main feelings, it was probably a Punitive Parent Mode.

Try to sense what the voice of your Parent Mode was like. Does its "tone" sound familiar to you? Often, people have a spontaneous idea about where this Mode originates from in childhood. They know the person that this voice arises from. If you understand the roots of the Dysfunctional Parent Mode it will be easier to do the exercises later in this chapter, which are all about silencing that voice.

We strongly recommend that, in contrast to the imagery exercises you may have used to deal with Vulnerable Child Modes, you really shouldn't get *into* the Punitive, Guilt-inducing, or Demanding voices of your Parent Mode. Stay on a cognitive and rational level when you first try out these exercises. In other words, don't try to relive feelings very intensely. After you've gone through the process of collecting first experiences you may intensify the mental images. But be careful – beware of becoming overwhelmed by the feelings of these Modes! In particular, strong Punitive Parent Modes can easily take "emotional command" and make you feel very low very quickly. If you sense that distressing feelings are overwhelming you, think about someone you can talk with about the experience. This should reassure you and calm you down.

Particularly in strong Punitive Parent Modes we recommend that you deal with the following questions on a cognitive level – just think about them in the here and now.

Discriminate: Which rules and messages from your Healthy Adult Mode are helpful for your life today? Which ones are not helpful any more?

Exercise 9.2

What are the Messages of my Parent Mode and what is their Origin?

During our childhood and youth we usually face various demands regarding discipline, achievement, modesty etc. Sometimes we hear specific sentences over and over again and they seem to become "burnt" into our memory – slogans such as "No Pain, No Gain," proverbs like "The early bird catches the worm." Maybe there was an authority figure who kept on at you with the same, typical sentence – something such as "Do I have to get mad at you again?" People with a Punitive Parent Mode often have memories of insulting nicknames. One of our patients for example was always being called "Mr Hopeless" by his father.

Do you remember such messages? Make a list of the messages you got as a child or adolescent (Worksheet 13, "Identifying parent messages"). Which of these messages are still important to you today and which ones are not that strong? What do those messages mean for your life? How do you feel about them? How do you act in response and reaction to these messages today, and how do you feel about that?

Usually, some of the messages we get from parents and other authority figures are very helpful later in life. For example, most parents try to impart discipline. Although you may have found it annoying or boring from time to time, on the whole you've benefited from it. You have learned to keep going when things are difficult, and that it's not always possible to do what you like. Very likely you are a good parent yourself today because you learnt from your parents that it is important to care for others.

In the schema Mode concept, such "good" messages are part of the Healthy Adult part of you. They help you to perform well and to adhere to important social rules (see Chapter 5). Most adults

Worksheet 13: Identifying Parent Messages

Identifying Parent Messages

Message of the Parent Mode:	Origin of this message:	How strong is the impact of this message today?(0–100)	When does this Mode get activated?
To do something just for yourself is egoistic.	My mother used to sacrifice her life for others (role Model)	Impact today: 85	As soon as I try to allow myself something

have benefited from the positive and negative messages given out by their parents.

Nevertheless, there are also messages from the past that put pressure on you without being helpful to you or anybody else. This applies in particular to the self-devaluing messages of the Punitive Parent Mode. The influence of those messages has to be reduced because they only make you feel bad. As so often, it's about finding a happy medium – discipline and healthy self-criticism are good; but perpetual self-criticism or punishing yourself harshly for normal mistakes is damaging and only makes you unhappy.

It is important that you figure out which of your "parent messages" belong to the Healthy Adult and which are part of the Punitive, Demanding or Guilt-inducing Parent Modes. Worksheet 14, "My parent messages," will help you with this. You need to be familiar

Worksheet 14: My Parent Messages

My Parent Messages		
Parent message	*Biographic origin*	*Mode*
(1)		
(2)		
(3)		
(4)		
(5)		

with the Modes described in the first part of this book before you start on this worksheet (see Chapters 3 and 5).

After discriminating between messages from the Healthy Adult and Dysfunctional Parent Modes you should decide which of these messages you want to carry on receiving and which you want to cut right back. Aim to keep the messages of the Healthy Adult Mode and to put onto the change agenda those messages that are putting pressure on you or giving you a bad feeling about yourself. In addition, you should start to adopt healthier, more moderate rules for messages in need of revision (see Section 2.1.2).

Figure 9.1   Overcoming Parent Modes

Case Example

In the beginning of Chapter 3 you got to know Aisha, Annabelle, and Freddie, who all suffer from different types of Parent Modes. All of them were able to identify different messages emanating from their damaging Parent Modes:

Aisha's parental messages	Biographic origin	Mode
If you don't take care of others you are a bad person	Mother	Guilt-inducing Parent Mode
Your feelings and needs do not matter	Mother	Punitive Parent Mode
You can reach your goals if you make an effort.	Teacher, father	Healthy Adult Mode

Aisha decided to change the first parental message. She intends to replace it by the rule "It's good to take care of others but your needs are also important. I want to find a good balance." in the future. The second parental message should just be erased since it does not help Aisha or anybody else at all. Aisha senses that the third rule does not make excessive demands and therefore is related to her Healthy Adult Mode. It should continue to play an important role in her life.

Annabelle's parental messages	Biographic origin	Mode
You don't deserve good food	Nuns	Punitive Parent Mode
You don't deserve pleasure	Nuns	Punitive Parent Mode
Your need for fun is bad	Nuns	Punitive Parent Mode
You are a loser when you make a mistake	Nuns	Punitive Parent Mode

The messages that Annabelle picked up from the nuns deny her needs, her emotions, and the right to care well for herself. They make her hate and reject her body and her needs. She decides to work on erasing and replacing of all these messages to help her develop self-compassion and a more satisfying life.

Freddie's parental messages	Biographic origin	Mode
Business before pleasure	Parents as role models	Demanding Parent Modes
It's important that you feel good	Parents' statements	Healthy Adult Mode

Freddie gets messages from his Demanding Parent Mode driving him to high achievement and diligence at work. However, his parents also taught him to be interested in other things beside his job and that he should always look after himself. Therefore, Freddie has a strong Healthy Adult Mode alongside his Demanding Parent Mode.

His aim is to reduce the weight of his Demanding Parent Mode messages to some degree. In the future it should be: "Work is important and it's a good thing to be successful. But it's also important to keep a balance – there are other important things in life besides your job."

9.2   Silence Dysfunctional Parent Modes

Now we're going to teach you the ways to change Dysfunctional Parent Modes. First, you have to revise the rules that apply to your damaging Parent Mode to define new, healthy rules. Then you must learn to answer back to the Dysfunctional Parent Mode messages with your new rules – step by step your answers will become louder and the influence of the damaging messages will be reduced – they may even become silenced.

Find new life rules. How can you replace the rules of your Dysfunctional Parent Mode with healthier messages? In Worksheet 15, "Collecting Messages against the Damaging Parent Mode" you will find two examples. Try to add some of your own.

Worksheet 15: Collecting Messages against the Damaging Parent Mode

Collecting Messages against the Damaging Parent Mode	
Message of my Damaging Parent Mode	*Personal proof against this message*
You are bad if you don't take care of others.	It's important to support others. To do so, it's important to take care of myself, too.
Business before pleasure	It is important to deal with assignments responsibly. However, I have to make sure that I allow myself pleasures from time to time for a good balance in life.

How much truth is there in your parent messages? After starting to deal with your Parent Mode you may well begin to wonder whether your Dysfunctional Parent Mode isn't right after all. Such doubts are completely normal. The Dysfunctional Parent Mode has been part of your life and of your self-perception for many years. People with a strong Punitive Parent Mode develop a tendency to perceive themselves and others as if the Punitive Parent Mode was right. Psychologists call this phenomenon **selective perception**: you see proofs of only the negative messages about yourself and ignore the evidence supporting the positive messages. The following box gives an example.

Case Example

Abigail's Punitive Parent Mode tells her: "You are so ugly that you'll never find a partner." Ever since she started getting this message she's tended to interpret events and remarks as if this message were true. When she looks into the mirror, she only sees what she assumes to be – what she *knows* to be – a big nose. She does not notice her beautiful eyes and her lovely hair. Nor does she notice that her good friend and tennis partner has been in love with her for a long time.

Collect facts and arguments that you can set against your Guilt-inducing or Punitive Parent Mode. This may be difficult in the beginning, but stay tuned! You need a lot of practice before you can answer back effectively to a Punitive Parent Mode. Worksheet 15 will help you. When you're struggling, finding that this is too difficult to do on your own, ask a close friend to help you check the messages from your Parent Mode.

After you've decided which messages you want to diminish in influence, you face the challenging task of reducing the power of those messages. Which one is the first to take on?

9.2.1 Exercises to reduce Dysfunctional Parent Messages

- **Use the power of symbols.** It can be very helpful to carry a small item with you (e.g. a small puppet, a stone, a shell, a little Stop sign) as a symbol and reminder of your resistance to your damaging Parent Mode. It reminds you of your plan to answer back. For example, a small Stop sign on your desk may remind you to set limits, not to say "Yes" to every extra assignment.
- **Postcard or letter to yourself.** Write a postcard to yourself to **reinforce** your intention of diminishing the influence of a particular parental message. Emphasize that you have the right to change these things in your life!

Hey Isabella,

You are okay, and your needs are okay, too! At least that's what Molly, Joseph, Mia, and Emma think — and they should really know... ☺

- **Get support from others.** Such a postcard can be particularly powerful when others write it for you, acknowledging your needs. You might also put pictures of people who would answer back to your Parent Mode (e.g. your partner, family, friends) on your computer desktop to reinforce you every time you look at the screen.

If you have a very strong Punitive Parent Mode (such as Annabelle in Chapter 3) it may be difficult for you to do these exercises. Maybe your Punitive Parent Mode makes fun of you or doesn't allow you to act against it. Then you may feel guilty or even feel that your Punitive Parent Mode is gaining strength instead of weakening.

In such cases the support of others is extremely important. It can be very helpful to talk these topics through with someone. Often, professional support from a therapist is needed as well. You need real support from others, but you may use imagery exercises to increase the impact of their support. Many people do that quite automatically: when they're worried or upset about something they talk to supportive people in their imagination. Do you know that phenomenon? Mostly it happens automatically, but you can also try to generate, or retrieve from your past or current life, an "inner helper." Try to get in contact with your helper whenever your dysfunctional parent rises up or denies your emotions and needs. If you're not used to drawing on the support of such an "inner helper" you should definitely give it a try – it may be a big help!

Exercises 9.3

Exercises with the Inner Helper

The messages from your Punitive Parent Mode are probably very clear to you. Now, think about those people in your life who are self-compassionate and who stand by you and acknowledge your needs and your feelings. Who might have a very different image of you than the people who laid the ground for the Punitive Parent Mode? Maybe your grandmother or a loving aunt from your childhood; or it might be a current good friend or your partner. It's not necessary to choose a person who actually knew you when you were little.

When you've found your inner helper you can start dealing with a situation in the here and now where your Punitive Parent Mode is active. Maybe you're blaming yourself for strains in your intimate relationship, although the problems are is not all your fault and you would be well advised to be lenient towards yourself. Or do you hate yourself for gaining a couple of pounds during the holidays? Or do you feel ridiculous as soon as you open your mouth in public?

When you find yourself in such a situation, imagine telling your inner helper about it. It is very important to wait for the answers they give you. What does your inner helper say? Do the answers suggest that your inner helper generally accepts your needs and feelings and looks at you in a loving way? If that's not the case, it's probably your Punitive Parent Mode again. If this keeps happening it's probably better to address these issues in psychotherapy. But if you sense that the answers from your inner helper are actually supportive and helpful you can take the next step and do an imagery exercise.

Imagine a situation where your Punitive Parent Mode is active. Now, let your inner helper enter the situation in your imagination. How does that feel? What do you need to join in, in your imagination, to further weaken the influence of the Punitive Parent Mode?

It will certainly take some time to change Dysfunctional Parent Modes. But it's worth it – you will notice that you're getting more relaxed and you'll see how you can accept your needs once you've decided that you'll no longer tolerate these Modes. Keep in mind that normal problems and crises in anyone's life (e.g. problems in your marriage or your job) are usually accompanied by the rise of Dysfunctional Parent Modes. That's normal and shouldn't discourage you from following this path!

10

Changing Coping Modes

As with all other Modes, the important first step is to understand your Coping Modes thoroughly. The best way to do this is to think hard about your thoughts, feelings, and actions and to ask trustworthy people for their views on the way you seem to cope. The trustworthy people might include your therapist but might just be your friends, your partner, your siblings, or your favorite colleagues. Moreover, you should reflect on feedback you've previously had. Have other people, for example. noticed and commented that you've got a habit of trying to get around important things (Avoidant Coping Mode)? Or have you been asked repeatedly why you let other people treat you badly, or why you tolerate unbearable situations (Compliant Surrender Coping Mode)? Have you been accused of being arrogant or too aggressive (Overcompensating Coping Mode)? Comments of this kind are a precious source of information about your Coping Modes. Since we often feel quite well when we are in a Coping Mode, neutral observers are sometimes better than we are ourselves at detecting our typical coping behaviors. However, that will change once you've come to understand your Coping Modes; then it will be much easier for you to identify the Coping Mode you just "slipped into."

Breaking Negative Thinking Patterns: A Schema Therapy Self-Help and Support Book,
First Edition. Gitta Jacob, Hannie van Genderen and Laura Seebauer.
© 2011 Beltz Psychologie in der Verlagsgruppe
Beltz • Weinheim Basel. Published 2015 by John Wiley & Sons, Ltd.

10.1   Get in Touch with your Coping Modes

The following questions will help you determine your Coping Modes:

- What kind of feedback do you get from friends or colleagues?
- Do people from different life contexts (e.g. work, leisure, family) notice similar behavior patterns in you?
- How do you react to emotional distress, e.g. conflicts in your relationships or at work?
- Which coping styles from Chapter 4 did you recognize in yourself?
- Go to your friends, your partner, or other people to you and ask them directly which coping style they associate with you. They'll probably have good reasons for their opinions – but maybe they'll never tell you unless you ask.

Keep in mind that Surrendering and Avoidant Coping behaviors are relatively easy to detect. People with these coping styles often sense clearly that they have emotional difficulties in dealing with certain situations. Things are different for overcompensation. When you are stuck in an overcompensatory Mode, showing off or attacking others, you may feel really strong and well in yourself. Negative feelings are pushed aside.. People around you can see, maybe even see through, your behavior but don't dare to confront you. Therefore, it is often difficult to gain insight into your own overcompensation. An imagery exercise (Exercise 10.1) can be helpful.

10.2   Reducing Coping Modes

The main goal here is to modify, in fact, to weaken, your Coping Modes in a way that stops them standing in your way when you're trying to meet your needs. It's important to keep in mind that every Coping Mode has a purpose, and a sensible degree of coping is actually quite healthy. For example, in the midst of some desperate conflict at your workplace it's good to keep some

Exercise 10.1

This imagery exercise can be helpful when you are not sure about the origin of a surrendering or some other coping style.

Close your eyes and go back to a situation in which your Coping Mode was active. Put yourself into this situation in your imagination: What are you doing? How does your voice sound? What do you say? How do you feel? How does your body feel?

Once you've got in touch with the situation, build an **affective bridge** into your childhood memories. Let your mind wander into your childhood and adolescence. Do you see any images with your inner eye? What people, situations, feelings, and needs are related to these images? Get a feeling for the biographical situation.

Finish the exercise by reflecting on the connections between your feelings today and your childhood memories. What did you learn with the exercise? What questions are still unanswered?

Case Examples

1. Lots of times Karin has heard her husband and close friends say something along these lines: "There you go again: backing down and keeping out of everything." This comment is a dead give-away that Karin has a strong Avoidant Coping Mode, which goes along with social retreat. When she starts thinking about a recent conflict with her neighbor she notices that, indeed, she got around the confrontation by avoiding the neighbor for several weeks. *To get a better understanding of which situations trigger this Mode, she asks her husband and a*

friend who's often given her the same feedback to identify the events and difficulties that she's inclined to avoid.

2. Lora is a selfless and devoted nurse. She's often been told by her colleagues that she shouldn't always take on the extra assignments nobody wants to take. Some of her colleagues never agree to do the extra duties because they know that Lora will give in eventually. This sounds like a Compliant Surrender Coping Mode – presumably Lora feels so much pressure when there's a new assignment that she can't help surrendering to the demands. Instead of keeping within reasonable limits as regards work time and effort she gives in and extends her hours of work almost indefinitely. Indeed, she's spending so much time at work that she's lost sight of all her friends. *When she finally takes two weeks of vacation –only because her bosses pressured her to do so – she realizes that she's completely neglected her private life.*

3. You already know Glenn, the narcissistic doctor from Section 4.3. His wife has often complained about his narcissism. Now she reads about coping styles and shows him an article about overcompensation. Along with the article she asks him to think about this carefully.

Glenn reads the article and is outraged – who does she think she is? *At night he gets a beer and starts thinking about the whole issue. He has to admit that she has a point – it's true, for instance, that he feels very bad, rejected, when his colleagues get more credit than he does. When that happens he usually resorts to boasting about own achievements. However, when his wife raises the issue with him again, some days later, he pretends not to remember the article or what it was about.*

emotional distance and to be able to switch on some level of Avoidant Coping. Coping Modes become problematic when they cause harm in your life, because you can't manage to get out of them even if you want to.

Look at the pros and cons of your coping. Work out the advantages and disadvantages of your Coping Mode. First, try to get some feeling of when your Coping Mode causes problems and when it is actually useful. A pro–con list can be really helpful here. A pro–con list consists of two columns. The left is the "pro side": in this column you write down all the advantages of your Coping Mode. The right is the "con side": here you put all its disadvantages.

You may remember Harry, the insecure student of economics (Sections 4.2.1 and 4.2.2), and you have just been reading and thinking about Glenn. In the following box you will find the pro–con list for Harry's Avoidant Coping Mode and for Glenn's Overcompensation Mode (see 4.3.). Look at these lists and then use Worksheet 16, "Pros and cons of my Coping Mode" to check your own Coping Mode. Very often you find it's short-term advantages on the pro side and long term problems on the con side (**problematic behaviors**).

Harry's Avoidant Coping Mode

Pro	*Con*
I don't risk disappointment. If I don't attend exams, I don't risk failure.	I don't give my colleagues a chance to treat me better than my former classmates.
I protect myself against being hurt because I don't have close contacts or an intimate relationship.	I cannot experience the pleasure of being accepted or liked.
I can escape confrontation with my insecure feelings; while watching TV I feel safe and independent.	I don't have a girlfriend although I really want one.
I get around comparing myself to others.	I can't pursue my goals (e.g. finishing my studies) because I avoid exams.
	Because I never risk anything, I can't gain (friends, good achievements). This keeps my self-esteem at a very low level.

Glenn's Overcompensatory Coping Mode

Pros	Cons
I feel good and superior in the moment.	My colleagues don't like me.
I get respect and others don't dare to criticize or question me.	In a critical situation I'm pretty sure that none of my colleagues would stand behind me.
My appearance is a self-fulfilling prophecy, meaning that others regard me as more competent than I actually am.	My wife is annoyed by my "affectation."
	I actually still feel insecure when I compare myself to my colleagues.

Worksheet 16: Pros and Cons of my Coping Mode

Pros and Cons of my Coping Mode		
Coping style	Advantages	Disadvantages
My coping style:		
My coping style:		
My coping style:		
My coping style:		
My coping style:		
My coping style:		

These two examples should give you a picture of which life domain's Coping Modes can be particularly harmful and damaging. Moreover, they point to opportunities for change. They make it clear, too, that advantages and disadvantages are often quite closely balanced – at least from a short-term perspective. Unlike the way we dealt with Punitive Parent Modes, therefore, it is not the aim to simply erase your Coping Mode... It should be weakened, but not disappear completely.

Planning change. Where do you want to start in reducing the influence of your Coping Modes? Do you want to communicate more in a Healthy Adult Mode or do you want to show your feelings more directly? Is your first aim to express needs and limits more clearly? You will often start by seeking to change the patterns of your private or professional relationships.

Case Example

Harry's change plans:

- I want to confront myself with classes and exams at university.
- I will make an appointment with my professor next week to talk about my postgraduate ambitions.
- I want to get acquainted with at least two other students in order to feel less alone at university.
- Two nights a week I don't want to be on my own at home.

If you want to change your Coping Modes it's generally good to know how to activate your Healthy Adult Mode (see Chapter 5). Many people are in close contact with themselves and their Healthy Adult part when they take part in making music with others, such as by singing in a choir. Then they do neither avoid nor overcompensate. Other people feel most secure (and do not need to rely on a Coping Mode) when dealing with children or animals.

Once you know the kind of situations where you don't need any kind of Coping Mode, you should be able to use them to get along better in other situations as well. You should use the "coping-free" situations as an inner "safe place."

For the following exercise you need to imagine two situations – one "safe situation" in which you do not need a Coping Mode, and another more difficult situation in which you would normally be likely to react with your dominant Coping Mode.

Exercise 10.2

First, enter the safe situation in your imagination – singing in the choir, or playing with animals. How do you feel? Try to experience these relaxed and safe feelings intensively. Next, enter the difficult situation in your imagination and try to take along the feelings of safety and relaxation. Maybe you can also take along someone who was involved in the safe situation.

Note whether this exercise can change your feelings in the difficult situation, even if it's only slightly.

10.2.1 Reducing the Compliant Surrender Mode

After you set up your change schedule you should choose to address some concrete situation. Maybe you've got a colleague who has been annoying you with an irritating habit for ages and you would like to ask her to stop it. Or you'd like to get your family members involved in some tasks that you've been doing on your own for a long time? Keep in mind that change always takes small steps. Start with changing one minor thing and continue from there.

10.2.2 Reducing avoidance

Reducing avoidant behavior can be quite a task. Surrendering in a situation is always a short-term relief; thus, you always benefit in the short run from surrendering. (However, it causes big long-term problems. It can be a huge relief not to surrender!)

Exercise 10.3

Reducing the Compliant Surrender Mode

You should plan concrete, realistic, and small steps when you start changing things. Furthermore, you need some idea of what your alternative behavior should be. How would you actually like to act in this situation? Don't just aim to put a stop to your coping behavior, go on to develop a positive "vision" of your change – this is actually more important!

As a first step, imagine your new behavior vividly in an imagery exercise:

Make yourself comfortable and close your eyes.

Take pleasure in imagining how you act in a new way. If you feel your conscience beginning to raise objections to the new you try to determine if it's your Guilt-inducing or Punitive Parent Mode. If yes, oppose to this Mode with a clear message –for example, "I don't want you to play a big role in my life any more! Get out of this imagery exercise!"

The next step is to implement your "vision" in a relatively undemanding situation. Don't be disappointed if it doesn't work out perfectly on the very first try. At least you tried, that's already a success! And a small step is a good step.

Next, start to implement your new behavior in more situations in your daily life. Reward yourself for progress. Praise yourself or give yourself a pat on the back... Or you may grant yourself a bowl of ice cream, a relaxing bath or a little present!

Case Example

Joshua (Chapter 4) decided to reduce the influence of his Compliant Surrender Mode. He already has an idea where to start. One client always manages to burden him with annoying assignments that are actually not part of his job. In the next meeting Joshua manages to resist the pressure to offer his support. When the client asks him for help, he declines in a friendly tone of voice. After the meeting he feels relieved and looks forward to acting in this way more often.

Unfortunately, this is often not true with Avoidance Coping Mode. When you start doing things that you've been avoiding it's likely that you will find the process extremely stressful. The positive reward comes only after some time. You need patience and consistency to change avoiding behavior patterns!

Your pro and con list is very important here, too, because it helps you to keep the long-term disadvantages of avoidance in the front of your mind. This may support and strengthen your motivation for change. The reduction and weakening of avoidance follows the same rules as for surrendering (see Exercise 10.2 and Worksheet 16, "Pros and cons of my Coping Mode"). You can also use an imagery exercise like 10.3 in this case.

Figure 10.1   Reducing avoidance

Case Example

Harry decided to get in touch with his fellow students. When the next party is announced he works up his courage and agrees to come. At the party night he finally shows up around 11 p.m. He hardly sees any familiar faces and most people are already quite drunk. Harry ends up standing alone in the host's kitchen, feeling uncomfortable and unconnected. He only briefly talks to a fellow student who is also interested in computer games. Unfortunately that guy leaves the party soon, as he has to work the next day. Harry feels his Punitive Parent Mode reaching up with the message "You're just not one of them."

When he finally leaves the party he feels disappointed and exhausted. But the next week he bumps into the guy he met at the party and he invites Harry to come over and play computer games with some friends. Harry accepts the invitation and notices that he feels much better meeting and interacting with a small number of people. He feels good about talking to the other guys and gaming with them.

10.2.3 Reducing Overcompensation

The reduction of overcompensation is similar to the reduction of Surrendering and Avoidant Mode patterns. However, probably even more than in the reduction of avoidance, the reduction of overcompensation will start to pay off only after some time. At first, you may well feel worse without your overcompensatory patterns. That is why it is so challenging to reduce overcompensation.

You've been coping with feelings of inferiority or anxiety by showing off or reacting aggressively. But you've managed to identify your overcompensatory coping style and decided to reduce it. The first time you don't show off you may find yourself in touch with your feelings of inferiority. You may well feel more miserable since you're no longer hiding behind your Coping Mode. And apart from that, showing off often feels great! It makes you feel satisfied, strong, and dominant.

You have to do without these good feelings if you want to change your pattern. Eventually, though, you'll probably notice how much the people around you disliked your showing-off…

All these experiences will be worthwhile and important for you in the long term – although at first they may feel very bad. You can be proud of yourself when you manage to reduce overcompensation!

Understandably, people are usually only motivated to reduce overcompensation if they experience some disadvantages from it – other people drawing back, or their partner threatening to leave them. If you're going through this process you may become depressed or anxious at first. This may sound harsh, but experience has shown that it's true: negative experiences with overcompensation can *increase* your chances of a successful reduction of overcompensation. They can motivate your change! You may not start working on your overcompensation without the spur of such negative consequences – as long as people accommodate themselves to your wishes, you probably won't consider changing your ways.

Figure 10.2   Reducing overcompensation

Case Example

Thomas has been fighting severe feelings of inferiority and shame for the last 20 or 30 years. These feelings origin from his adolescence – he was mocked and bullied at school because of his severe acne. To cope, he developed a strong Overcompensatory Coping Mode. In this Mode he behaves extremely coolly and competently, dazzles others with his rugged good looks, and is endlessly efficient in his work.

Today, Thomas is 47 years old and no longer has quite the energy he had when he was young. He realizes that his coping style is exhausting him. Moreover his work situation has changed: the assignments are smaller nowadays and his perfect looks aren't helping him in the way they used to. He feels burdened and sees no way out. He has developed severe depressive symptoms over the last few years.

His therapist points out his overcompensation to him. For Thomas this was a tough nut to crack. Nevertheless, he finds the topic worth working on it. He tries to cut down his "smart-ass" comments in therapy and instead starts to deal with his negative feelings. At work he starts experimenting with being more open about his abilities. To do so he has to say good-bye to the illusion of never-ending capacity. Instead of working all night as he used to he starts telling his boss when he needs more time for an assignment.

Thomas finds this change very hard, and feels threatened when he opens up and shows his weaknesses. However, overall it's a good experiences; it's a relief to be understood by others and to be given support. Best of all, he does not feel quite so alone.

When you tend to show aggressive overcompensation, your Coping Mode is probably a strong protection against feeling weak or helpless. If you intend to reduce overcompensation, you have to find new ways of protecting yourself. Everyone needs to feel protected in difficult situations. Don't expect too much of yourself and forgive yourself if you fall back into an overcompensatory pattern – nobody is perfect at the first attempt. What matters is to persist.

Case Example

Carolyn (see Section 4.3.) has had many conflicts due to her Aggressive Coping Mode. She's even had some encounters with the police. Thus, she has good reason to change her aggressive coping. However, when she tries to act less aggressively she feels more helpless and abandoned than before. She certainly won't be able to stop her aggressive reactions overnight.

Carolyn learns to talk with others about her Coping Mode. This turns out to be her way out. In distressing situations she sometimes has to take a deep breath as she senses her Aggressive Coping Mode stirring. After some time she's learned to say in such situations (sometimes to another person, but often just to herself): "Wait a minute. I feel my aggression rising. Just give me one minute to breathe." Obviously, the people and institutions in her environment are very happy with her change and are willing to give her the time she needs to "cool down." As time goes by. Carolyn improves her healthy and non-aggressive reactions step by step.

Worksheet 17, "Changing my Coping Mode," will help you to reduce your Coping Mode in small steps. Why not start today?

Hopefully, this chapter has helped you to understand where your Coping Modes originate, which coping mechanisms are most important for you and what steps you can take to reduce them. Maybe it is a bit frightening in the beginning to be more strongly in your Healthy Adult Mode in some situations. That's perfectly normal; the fear will fall away quite soon if you stick to the job! The more you exercise, the more you will notice how good it feels to express your emotions, needs, and limits in a clear and healthy way. Ask others who are close to you if they noticed a change in you, and what they think about it. Feedback from other people is extremely important to the success of your efforts to reflect your patterns and how they affect others.

Worksheet 17: Changing my Coping Mode

Changing my Coping Mode
I want to reduce my Coping Mode in the following situation:
I used to act like this (Coping Mode):
I want to change that, because ... (disadvantages of the Coping Mode):
Instead my Healthy Adult Mode wants to act as follows:
This is how I'm going to reward myself when I make it:

11

Promoting Your Healthy Adult Mode

As you read this chapter you may start to think that it's repeating issues from the earlier chapters, and you'd be absolutely right! The Healthy Adult part of you is needed for all changes to all the other Modes. Let's summarize: Vulnerable Child Mode should be comforted and strengthened; Angry Child Modes should be given the opportunity to express their emotions and needs more adequately; Impulsive or Spoilt Child Modes must learn to tolerate reasonable limits; Avoidant Coping Modes should be reduced; and Punitive, Guilt-inducing, or Demanding Parent Modes have to be neutralized. All these developments are driven by your Healthy Adult Mode: the Healthy Adult part of you comforts the Vulnerable Child, sets limits to the spoilt child, negotiates with coping, and silences the Parent Modes. Thus, your Healthy Adult Mode is vital for all the changes you might wish to achieve.

Now it's up to your Healthy Adult part to set priorities. Which change seems most important to you and how much energy do you want to put into the process? How will you reward yourself when you've made the first steps? Reflecting on these issues is an important exercise for your Healthy Adult Mode. Don't over-burden yourself, as your Demanding Parent Mode asks of you. Accept that you can't get everything at once, as the Undisciplined Child may suggest. Unfortunately, the Vulnerable Child elements may not get all the care they might need, even if you manage to

Breaking Negative Thinking Patterns: A Schema Therapy Self-Help and Support Book,
First Edition. Gitta Jacob, Hannie van Genderen and Laura Seebauer.
© 2011 Beltz Psychologie in der Verlagsgruppe
Beltz • Weinheim Basel. Published 2015 by John Wiley & Sons, Ltd.

take better care of them… Again, it's the job of the Healthy Adult Mode to recognize limits and to stay level-headed. The following ideas may help you to set up a realistic change schedule.

Role models. Fortunately, most people have someone, or several people, who can serve as role models for Healthy Adult behavior. We dealt with this topic in Chapter 9. Who will listen to you and understand your sorrows when you are sad or upset? Who looks at you affectionately? Who do you know that can manage and balance his or her own needs *and* the interests of others?

Often, such models are real people – maybe your aunt, your grandmother, or a close friend. But if you don't know a real person who fits as a role model you can perfectly easily use a character from a story or a movie instead. It's important to have someone at your side who is both warm-hearted and realistic.

If you feel that adopting such a perspective is very difficult for you, you are not a failure. It might be a good idea, however, to see a professional therapist as a source of support for your Healthy Adult part.

Be realistic. Life isn't perfect, and human-beings aren't perfect either. This is no reason to become desperate – it's completely normal. You should always keep this in mind. Don't expect to fly to the stars, don't plan a day that would actually need 60 hours. Being realistic includes taking your true potential into account – no matter whether you are focusing on your social contacts, your job, or your finances. You should always deal with actual, existing conditions and plan how to get the best out of them. Being realistic also means acknowledging that there are better and worse phases in your life: you're not going to get a perfect personal balance every time. Accept your limits and the ups and downs of your life; aim to get your needs met as fully as possible under the circumstances. It is also part of being realistic to review and act within your power to change a situation at all. Imagine that you want to change the conflicts you have with your boss. It may well be that after careful consideration you have to accept that your boss is just too difficult to change, or that you'd have to

put up with unbearable conditions at work to stop the conflicts…
In such situations the realistic action is either put a lot more distance between you and your boss, or look for another job.

Be honest with yourself. Often, people want to change a lot in
their life. However, change demands a lot of effort. For instance,
it will take many years to make a wish for a university degree
come true. It will certainly be positive for your mental and
physical health to pursue a healthier lifestyle – healthier eating,
losing weight, quitting smoking, or exercising more. But keep in
mind that you'll need a lot of discipline and effort. You will only
reach goals like these if you are motivated and mobilize a lot of
energy. Some dream bubbles may burst when you ask yourself if
you're honestly ready. Being honest with yourself is important: if
you're not honest you'll likely end up chronically frustrated and
dissatisfied (and of course you won't reach your goals).

Find a balance between your needs and the needs of others.
All the chapters in this book deal in some way with the question
of how you can manage to get your needs met. But, of course, you
have to realize that others have their needs, too. The limit to our
freedom is always the freedom of others. It's usually possible to
find a compromise and we should always be ready to meet people
halfway.

When people finally start paying attention to their own
needs, it can be quite irritating for others in their circle. Other
people may just not be used to it. It's important to watch carefully the steps you're making. Give the people around you
some time to get accustomed to your change. For instance, if
you've never before "shocked" your husband by taking up
activities on your own, don't start too many of them overnight!
Give him some time to get used to the new you… If you sense
that someone important in your life is irritated or annoyed,
just take your time with your development –they'll probably
get used to it after a while. If they don't, though, you may
decide to talk things over and explain your new behavior.
Maybe this is a time for working out a compromise (see
above)…

Get concrete. Many people spend years longing for some change in their life. However, their ideas are often vague – "I'd like to be more self-confident," "I need a better balance in my life," or "I want to care more for myself." These are good, useful goals, but they're also too vague and too universal. Our experience as therapists has taught us that the more concrete your goals, and the closer those goals are to your actual behavior, the higher the probability of realizing them.

The following questions guide you towards becoming more concrete about one popular personal goal – "I want to be more self-confident":

- What does it look like to be self-confident?
- How can I recognize that somebody is self-confident? How does he or she actually behave? What makes me realize that this person is self-confident?
- In which situations do I want to be more self-confident? What would it look like if I behaved self-confidently in this situation? What would make other people realize it? What is the difference the ideal and my current behavior in this situation?

Worksheet 18, "Changes" can help you to set priorities and to get a realistic view of your possibilities.

Imagery exercises. We've already been through several imagery exercises. They are an ideal way to strengthen your Healthy Adult Mode. To prepare yourself for change, you should imagine doing certain things in your Healthy Adult Mode (Exercise 11.1).

This sounds a little bit silly to many people when they first hear about it – but just give it a try! For many people an initial rehearsal in fantasy is a great preparation for real change.

Activities. To strengthen your Healthy Adult Mode you have to be aware of situations which help you to get into this Mode. This may not always be easy, especially when your Healthy Adult part is not very strong. If that is the case, you should give a high priority to scheduling activities that bring you closer to this Mode. The more you pursue such activities, the stronger your

Worksheet 18: Changes

Changes	(1)	(2)	(3)
I want to change the following things:			
How important is this change? (0–100)			
How much can I influence this change? (0–100)			
How motivated am I for this change? (0–100)			
Am I prepared to invest some effort to change? (0–100)			
What do I need to attain this goal?			
What do I need to make this goal more concrete?			
Who is affected by this change? What are the consequences?			

Exercise 11.1

Think of a particular situation where you usually back down but where you actually ought to pursue your interests. Start by imagining how you would like things to go (and how you'd like yourself to behave). Relax, close your eyes and run a film before your mind's eye. Imagine what it would be like to be in your Healthy Adult Mode in this situation.

Case Example

You already know Megan from Section 2.1. She and her family used to move around a lot in her childhood, so she was always "the new one" at school and in the neighborhood. This history makes Megan often still feel excluded. When this happens she feels sad and rejected (Vulnerable Child Mode) and is convinced that others don't want her to participate (Punitive Parent Mode).

In the imagery exercise Megan imagines a quite difficult situation. She visualizes some of her fellow students sharing a table at the cafeteria. They all sit together talking and laughing. In real life, Megan would choose to sit somewhere else by herself in such a situation, but in the imagery exercise she approaches the table and asks for permission to join them. The others agree, they make room for another chair and include her in the conversation.

The following week Megan encounters the real-life situation. Since she is prepared by her imagery exercise, she knows exactly how her Healthy Adult Mode would like to behave. She manages to join the group at the table. Afterwards she feels proud and happy.

Box 11.1

You can get into your Healthy Adult Mode if you...

- Learn something new
- Talk with a good friend about what matters in life
- Take responsibility for something
- Exercise
- Repair something
- Write down your positive experiences of the day at night
- Read a newspaper or a book
- Do something healthy (yoga, eating fresh fruits...)
- Try a new recipe
- Do a hobby
- Explain something to someone or help others
- Tick an item on your "to-do list" and reward yourself
- Write yourself a positive and friendly postcard

Healthy Adult Mode will become. Box 11.1 lists the kind of activities that evoke the Healthy Adult Mode.

Make a personal list of activities that bring up and promote your Healthy Adult Mode. It's a good idea to design your list nicely and give it a central place in your home so that you'll stumble across it from time to time. It is important to put concrete points on your Healthy Adult list, especially if you're aware that you tend to avoid Healthy Adult activities.

If your Healthy Adult Mode is already strong and often present, the following exercises may not be so relevant for you.

Behavior experiments. We explained behavior experiments in Section 7.2.3 dealing with the Angry Child Mode. Such experiments are a good way of approaching your Healthy Adult Mode. (Sometimes it is a good idea to access your Healthy Adult Mode in a light-hearted way.) Pick a specific situation in which you would like to behave in a Healthy Adult Mode (a situation where you need to pursue your interests) – even if you don't yet feel like it. An example would be if you felt insecure and anxious but still wanted to have a little chat with a colleague at your next meeting; then try out the approach and the chat as a behavior experiment.

Behavior experiments can vary a lot, depending on the behavior you want to change. Worksheet 19, "Behavior experiment" and the following case example can be a help.

Worksheet 19: Behavior Experiment

Behavior Experiment
Which situation do I want my Healthy Adult Mode to become the leader in?
How exactly do I want to behave?
Which Modes have been problematic so far?
What will help me to remind myself about my resolution in the situation (e.g. postcards, imagery exercise)?
How would a caring person encourage me?
How will I reward myself for success in the behavior experiment?

Case Example

You already know Susie from Section 2.2 and the beginning of Chapter 7. She has a strong Impulsive Child Mode in which she parties excessively, drinks too much alcohol, and ends up having unprotected sex. Susie's Impulsive Child Mode is a substantial threat to her studies and her health. She's realized by now that her Healthy Adult Mode has to take control of "party Susie" if she wants to finish her studies. She has not been going out for several weeks now to avoid temptation. However, she is missing contact with other people, music, and dancing. In this behavior experiment she wants to look for a balance between responsibility and fun.

She first writes down a message from her Healthy Adult Mode on a postcard:

Dear Susie,

At the party you will certainly be tempted to start drinking again and then go too far. Please keep in mind that your impulsive child gets her foot in the door as soon as you start drinking beer. Remember that your studies are important to you and that you cannot afford excessive partying! And I would like to remind you that this kind of behavior has put you in danger in the past... You're really too good for the guys you end up with.

As her behavior experiment Susie plans to go to a student party. So that her Healthy Adult Mode can stay in charge she isn't going to drink alcohol and she's going to go home at 1 a.m. at the latest. The card with the message from her Healthy Adult Mode is in her pocket. She's planned what to say when someone offers her alcohol and she's already tried it out in an imagery exercise.

It all works. This night Susie discovered that she can enjoy music and dancing even when she is not drunk. Moreover, she doesn't do things that she is ashamed of on the morning after. In fact, the next morning she is proud of herself and treats herself to a cappuccino and a chocolate cake in her favorite coffee shop.

This chapter is about the Healthy Adult Mode – the part in you that has an overview, sets priorities, stays realistic, accepts your needs, and brings them in balance with the needs of others. This is all quite demanding and no one can manage to be in this Mode all the time. However, if you often feel as if you almost don't have a Healthy Adult Mode it's important to accept it – but in such a case a (schema-) therapy will help you to promote and strengthen your healthy side.

Glossary

Affect, affective *Affect* is a synonym for *feeling* or *emotion*. The term *affective* covers all sensations and behaviors that are strongly influenced by feelings, closely attached to feelings or accompanied by emotional arousal.

Affective bridge An affective bridge is an association between a current situation and a situation in the past in which related emotions were present. Those situations don't need to be similar in content – it's all about the emotional connection. For instance, one could call it an affective bridge when the cool voice of your boss makes you panic, because that is the way your father sounded before he burst out in a rage attack.

Balance in social relationships Social psychologists investigate how people experience and form social relationships. Some studies have examined the contribution each partner makes in a relationship (e.g. how housekeeping tasks are distributed). They show that people systematically overestimate their own contribution in the relationship – on average by about 50 percent! So if you tend to say "in my relationship I take care of about two thirds to three quarters of stuff that needs to be done," you are very likely to live in an objectively balanced relationship in which each partner contributes 50 percent! Of course, this is just a rule of thumb that doesn't apply to every case. However, it does apply fairly often and it can be crucial to know this if you intend to be satisfied in a relationship.

Breaking Negative Thinking Patterns: A Schema Therapy Self-Help and Support Book,
First Edition. Gitta Jacob, Hannie van Genderen and Laura Seebauer.
© 2011 Beltz Psychologie in der Verlagsgruppe
Beltz • Weinheim Basel. Published 2015 by John Wiley & Sons, Ltd.

Bullying   Bullying means to physically agonize or emotionally hurt other people on a regular basis. This can take place at school, at work, in a sports club, or in the Internet. Mobbing has negative consequences for the victims' health, their job, and their private situation.

Coping   Coping is the way we deal with life events or a lifespan that we experience as important and difficult. People can have individual "coping strategies." These strategies can be either *functional* or *dysfunctional*. A functional coping means finding a sustainable, long-term solution for a problem. In contrast, dysfunctional coping often only provides short-term relief, the long-term problem persists.

Emotions, primary   Primary emotions are, first, those emotions that occur immediately after a stimulus. Primary emotions could be: joy, grief, anxiety, anger, surprise and disgust. Secondly, we call emotions "primary" in psychotherapy when they represent the "core" of a problem.

Emotions, secondary   Secondary (or social) emotions usually occur some time after a stimulus, and are "reactive" emotions, influenced by cognitive processes. Examples are: embarrassment, jealousy, guilt, shame, etc. A supplementary, psychotherapeutic definition is the following: sometimes other emotions than the "core" emotions are present (e.g. someone is nearly always railing against their partner, though they actually feel sad when the anger is gone); in this case sadness would be the primary emotion which is concealed by the secondary emotion, anger.

Hot emotions   Emotions are called "hot" if they go along with strong arousal and/or impulsive actions, such as rage, anger, or defiance.

Histrionic personality disorder   This disorder is characterized by theatrical, attention-seeking behavior. Affected individuals are often inappropriately seductive or provoking, show exaggerated self-presentation and a rapid change and dramatic expression of emotions, and are easily influenced.

Hysterical A hysterical personality is characterized by a specific dilemma: on the one hand they are afraid to make a commitment to something, on the other hand they long for stability. They are always active, seeking for new ideas and longing to be the center of attention. The hysterical personality is nowadays usually diagnosed as histrionic personality disorder with partly changed diagnostic criteria.

Needs Needs are impulses or urges that are important to an individual. Psychologists believe that several basic needs have to be fulfilled to live a satisfying and psychologically healthy life.

Parentification Switching of roles by parent and child because parents do not, often cannot, fulfill their commitment. The child is then overstrained because it has to perform a "parent role": the child has to take care of the well-being of family members although it's actually young to do so.

Problematic behavior A behavior is called *problematic* if it is pleasant in the short term but causes long-term problems. Typical problematic behaviors would be smoking or overeating – they provide short-term pleasure and satisfaction, but in the long term cause problems.

Procrastination Procrastination means to postpone, often indefinitely, necessary but unpleasant tasks.

Reinforcement A behavior is reinforced if a pleasant stimulus occurs as a consequence. This means that the behavior is rewarded and the probability that it will be repeated increases. For instance, if a small child manages to be given chocolate in response to an outburst of rage, it may well "produce" such outbursts more often in the future.

Selective perception To notice only those things that confirm your (negative) presumptions. You could also say you have "blinders on". An example would be someone who is giving a talk and who faces 50 interested viewers but notices in the back row two people keep chatting. If he feels that no one is interested in his talk he probably suffers from selective perception – he's blanked out the 50 interested viewers.

Vicarious learning   A learning process in which a person acquires new behavior by observing others. This can either be intended (e.g. if you imitate a certain movement which your trainer shows to you) or not intended (e.g. "bad role models").

References and Further Reading

American Psychiatric Association (2000). *Diagnostic and Statistical Manual of Mental disorders. DSM-IV-TR.* 4th edition, Text Revision. American Psychiatric Association: Washington, DC.

Arntz, A., & van Genderen, H. (2009). *Schema Therapy for Borderline Personality Disorder.* John Wiley & Sons: Chichester.

Arntz, A., Bernstein, D. P., & Jacob, G. (2013). *Schema Therapy in Practice. An Introductory Guide to the Schema Mode Approach.* John Wiley & Sons: Chichester.

First, M. B., Gibbon, M., Spitzer, R. L., Williams, J. B. W., & Benjamin, L. S. (1997). *Structured Clinical Interview for DSM-IV Axis II Personality Disorders, (SCID-II).* American Psychiatric Press: Washington, DC.

Young, J. E., & Klosko, J. S. (1993). *Reinventing Your Life: The Breakthrough Program to End Negative Behavior and Feel Great Again.* Penguin Books: Harmondsworth.

Young, J. E., Klosko, J. S., & Weishaar, M. E. (2003). *Schema Therapy: A Practitioner's Guide.* Guilford Press: New York.

Breaking Negative Thinking Patterns: A Schema Therapy Self-Help and Support Book,
First Edition. Gitta Jacob, Hannie van Genderen and Laura Seebauer.
© 2011 Beltz Psychologie in der Verlagsgruppe
Beltz • Weinheim Basel. Published 2015 by John Wiley & Sons, Ltd.

Index

Note: Page numbers in *italics* refer to Figures; those in **bold** to Tables

Breaking Negative Thinking Patterns: A Schema Therapy Self-Help and Support Book,
First Edition. Gitta Jacob, Hannie van Genderen and Laura Seebauer.
© 2011 Beltz Psychologie in der Verlagsgruppe
Beltz • Weinheim Basel. Published 2015 by John Wiley & Sons, Ltd.